How To Draw®

ENDANGERED ANIMALS

**Illustrated by
Georgene Griffin**

Visit us at www.kidsbooks.com

INTRODUCTION

This book will teach you how to draw many different types of animals. Some are more difficult to draw than others, but if you follow along, step by step, then (most important!) practice on your own, you soon will be able to draw these animals and others as you continue to learn about wildlife in danger. You also will learn the methods for drawing anything you want by breaking it down into basic shapes.

The most basic and commonly used shape is the oval. There are many variations of ovals: some are small and round, others are long and narrow, many are in between. Most of the figures in this book begin with some kind of oval. Then other shapes and lines are added to it to form the basic animal outline.

Most times, a free-form oval is used, like the ones pictured below. In addition to ovals, variations of other basic shapes—such as circles, squares, rectangles, triangles, and simple lines—are used to connect the shapes. Using these basic shapes will help you start your drawing.

Some basic oval and free-form shapes:

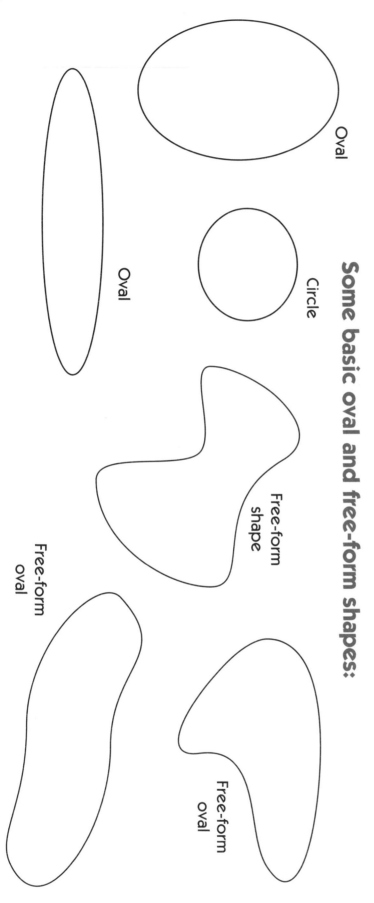

Oval

Circle

Free-form
shape

Oval

Free-form
oval

Free-form
oval

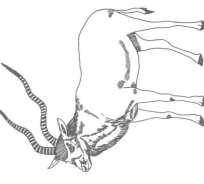

SUPPLIES

NUMBER-2 PENCILS
SOFT ERASER
DRAWING PAD

FELT-TIP PEN
COLORED PENCILS
MARKERS OR CRAYONS

HELPFUL HINTS

1. Take your time with steps 1 and 2. Following the first steps carefully will make the final steps easier. The first two steps create a solid foundation of the figure, much like a builder who must construct a foundation before building the rest of the house. Next comes the fun part—creating a smooth, clean outline drawing of the animal, then adding all the finishing touches, such as details, shading, and color.

2. Always keep your pencil lines light and soft. This will make the guidelines easier to erase when you no longer need them.

3. Don't be afraid to erase. It usually takes a lot of sketching and erasing before you will be satisfied with the way your drawing looks.

4. Add details, shading, and all the finishing touches only *after* you have blended and refined all the shapes and your figure is complete.

5. Remember: Practice makes perfect. Don't be discouraged if you don't get the hang of it right away. Just keep drawing, erasing, and redrawing until you do.

HOW TO START

Look at the finished drawing below, number 4. Study it. Then study the steps that were taken to get to the final drawing. Notice where the shapes overlap and where they align. Is the eye over the corner of the mouth or behind it? Look for relationships among the shapes.

Step 1. Draw the main shape first—usually, it is the largest. In this case, it is a large, free-form oval for the body. Then draw an overlapping oval for the hindquarters.

Step 2. Sketch additional basic shapes for the neck, head, legs and feet, and tail.

Step 3. Blend and refine the shapes to create a smooth outline of the animal's body. Keep erasing and drawing until you are satisfied.

Tip: Dotted lines indicate guidelines that you will erase when you no longer need them (in this case, in step 3).

Step 4. Add lots of lines for shading and fur texture, or color your drawing with colored pencils, markers, or crayons.

Sometimes, it is helpful to start by tracing the final drawing to get an overall sense of the its shape and size. Once you understand the relationships of the shapes and parts within the final drawing, you will find it easier to draw from scratch.

Remember: It is not important to get it perfect. It is important for you to be happy with your work!

Erasing Tips

● Once you have completed the line drawing (usually after step 2), erase unneeded guidelines. Then add details, shading, and/or coloring to your drawing.

● In the final stages, using a felt-tip marker over pencil lines you want to keep will make it easier to erase unneeded pencil lines.

● A very soft or kneaded eraser will erase the pencil lines without smudging the drawing or ripping the paper.

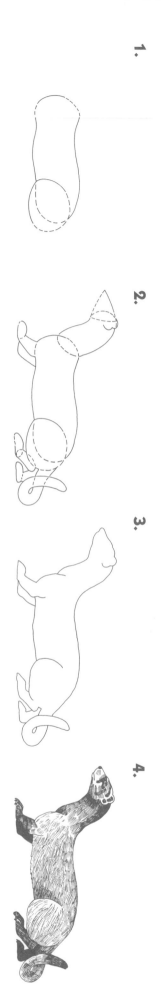

1.

2.

3.

4.

ABOUT ENDANGERED ANIMALS

The animals that you are about to meet and learn to draw may be different, but they all have one thing in common. They are endangered, which means that their numbers are declining to an alarmingly low level. Some are in danger of becoming extinct—disappearing from Earth—if humans do not make efforts to increase the animals' populations and preserve their habitats.

Why Are They Endangered?

There are many different reasons why a group of animals becomes endangered or threatened. Often, it happens from natural changes in Earth over time or from the effects that humans have on nature. Sometimes animals become endangered if a disease strikes suddenly and spreads.

Over thousands or millions of years, many types of animals become extinct. Sixty-five million years ago, dinosaurs disappeared from Earth. Scientists estimate that dinosaur species died off at a rate of only one species per 1,000 years. Today, they estimate, nearly 1,000 plant and animal species become extinct *each year!* In the last 300 years, more than 300 vertebrates (animals with backbones) have become extinct.

Humans have changed the world at a rapid pace. As the human population grows, people need more and more land for farms, homes, roads, and cities. Trees, and sometimes whole forests, are cut down, causing animals to lose their habitats and sources of food. Air and water pollution also take their toll. Hunters and trappers seek certain animals for food, skins and furs, and valuable trophies. This has caused many species to face extinction much sooner than they might in nature's own time.

What Is Being Done?

Now, more than ever, people are becoming aware of the plight of endangered animals and are working harder to preserve Earth's wild resources worldwide.

Here are some ways this is being done:

- Conservationists are increasing endangered species populations by breeding and raising them in captivity.
- When possible, conservationists are reintroducing endangered animals to their natural habitats.

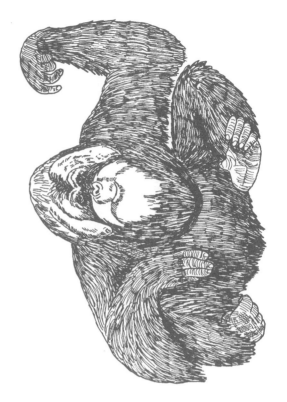

- Protected lands, such as national parks and animal preserves, have been set aside as places where wild animals can live without the threat of being hunted.
- Hunting is now regulated in most areas.
- More and more people are being educated about the vital role that all living things play in the well-being of our delicately balanced planet.

A Few Success Stories

The American alligator, the bison, and the bald eagle are all species that have returned from the brink of extinction, to the point where they are no longer considered endangered. The American alligator was once trapped for its valuable skin. The bison was once hunted for food and sport. The bald eagle became rare because the fish on which it fed contained the pesticide DDT. This chemical made the bald eagles' eggshells so thin that fewer and fewer eaglets were being born.

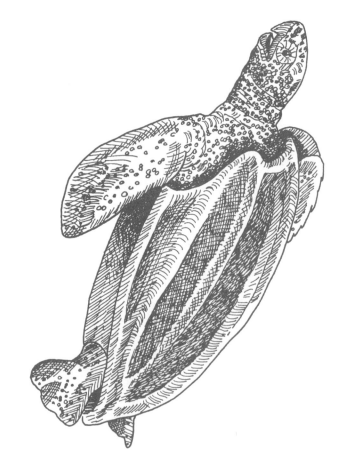

Today, thanks to the efforts of concerned people, the American alligator population has almost completely recovered, herds of bison once again roam areas of the American West, and DDT has been banned and the bald eagle is back.

What can you do to help save endangered animals? There are a number of things. One is that you can learn more about them. You can begin doing that right here—as you also learn how to draw them.

West Indian Manatee

This shy, gentle water mammal is also known as the sea cow. Spending its entire lifetime in warm, sheltered waters, a 12-foot manatee can eat up to 100 pounds of vegetation a day. The manatee can weigh up to 3,000 pounds, but has a 1-pound brain!

1. Begin with ovals for the body, head, snout, tail, and fins. Dotted lines will be erased, so draw them lightly.

Connect

Connect

Connect

Connect

2. Blend all the shapes together to form one long body shape from head to tail.

Flash fact: Today, manatees are protected but are still in danger. Many are maimed or killed by powerboats, which hit them as they swim close to the surface of the water.

3. Finish the manatee by adding an eye, nostril, whiskers, skin texture, and shading.

Bactrian Camel

A few wild herds of these two-humped camels exist in Mongolian parks and in the Gobi Desert. In both Mongolia and China, they are protected by law from hunting.

1. Start with a large, egg-shaped oval for the body. Add smaller ovals for the humps and head. Then add lines to connect the body and head. Be sure to sketch these basic shapes and lines lightly, since some of them will be erased later.

2. Next, add more ovals for the legs and feet. Draw the tail as shown.

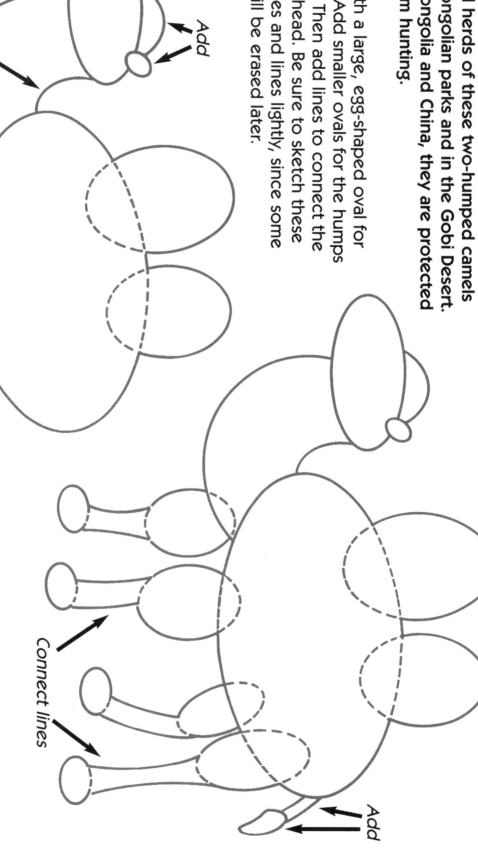

Add

Connecting lines

Connect lines

Add

Flash fact: Fewer than a thousand Bactrian camels survive in the wild today. One calf is born to an adult female every other year.

3. Blend all the roughed-out shapes into one body frame. Remember to erase any lines that you no longer need.

4. Add important details, such as the eye, ear, nose, and mouth. Complete your camel by sketching in lots of short lines to give its coat a shaggy look.

Tip: Keep erasing and drawing until you are satisfied.

Tiger

The biggest of all cats, tigers live in the wild only in Asia. Although overhunted for its beautiful coat, the tiger's greatest threat is loss of habitat. There are five times as many people living in the areas roamed by tigers than there were in 1900.

1. First, draw a large circle for the head. (Feel free to use a compass to help make it round.) Add two triangles at the top for ears and two simple, curving lines below for the upper body.

2. Next, sketch in two guideline shapes for the eyes, as shown. Add a triangle and three ovals as guidelines for the nose and mouth. Then sketch and erase to define the ears and upper body.

Tip: Dotted lines indicate guidelines that you will erase once you no longer need them.

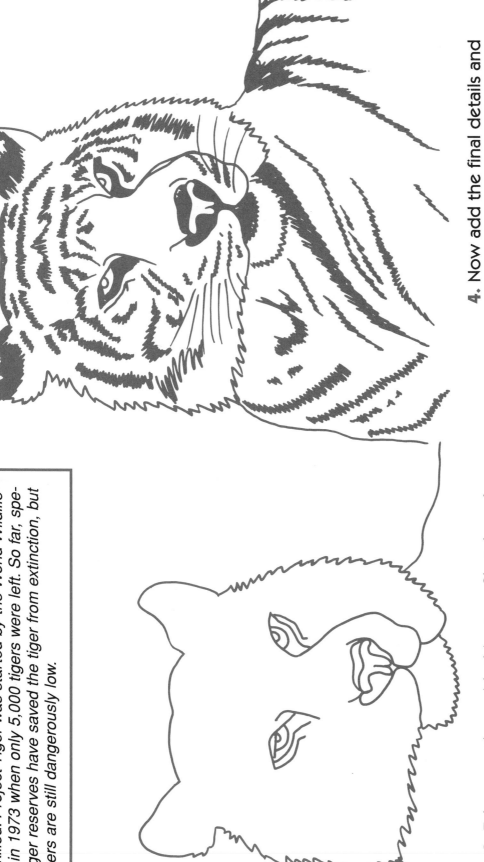

4. Now add the final details and finishing touches—especially those famous tiger stripes. (Did you know that a tiger's facial markings are as individual as human fingerprints?)

3. Take your time with this step. Sketch and erase to refine the shape of the head. (Notice how fur is created by using a jagged line around the head.) Start adding details to the facial features, erasing and redrawing until you get a smooth, clean outline, with each part the way you want it.

Giant Anteater

More and more South American grasslands are being grazed by cattle. This means fewer and fewer termite mounds, home to the giant anteater's favorite food.

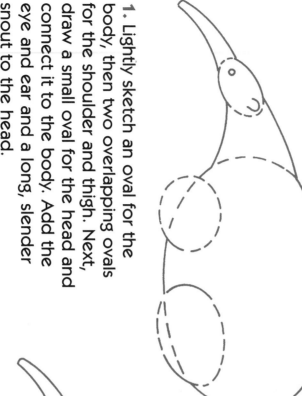

1. Lightly sketch an oval for the body, then two overlapping ovals for the shoulder and thigh. Next, draw a small oval for the head and connect it to the body. Add the eye and ear and a long, slender snout to the head.

2. Add more guidelines for the legs and paws, and a large free-form oval for the large, bushy tail. Now that the basic shapes have been completed, you can begin to refine your drawing.

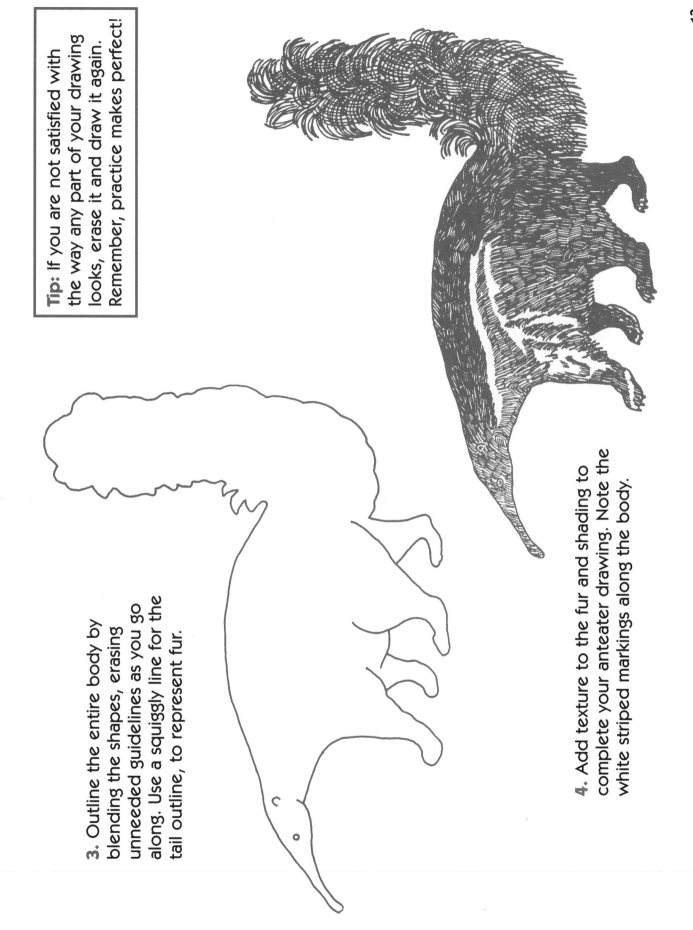

Tip: If you are not satisfied with the way any part of your drawing looks, erase it and draw it again. Remember, practice makes perfect!

3. Outline the entire body by blending the shapes, erasing unneeded guidelines as you go along. Use a squiggly line for the tail outline, to represent fur.

4. Add texture to the fur and shading to complete your anteater drawing. Note the white striped markings along the body.

Giant Panda

Giant pandas are very rare animals that live only in the forests of central China. They grow up to 5 feet in length and can weigh 300 pounds. These gentle animals are vegetarians. They consume 25 pounds of bamboo shoots and stems daily.

1. Draw a large oval for the panda's body, and smaller ones for the head, snout, nose, and ears.

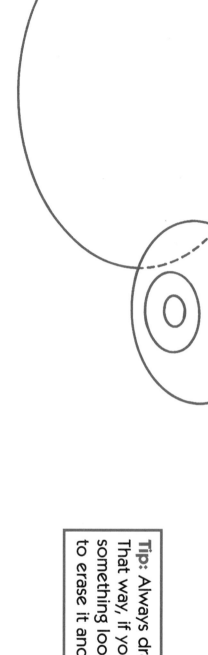

2. Add oval guidelines for the legs and paws.

Connect

Connect

Tip: Always draw guidelines lightly. That way, if you don't like the way something looks, it will be easier to erase it and try again.

3. Add shapes for the patches around the panda's mouth and eyes, then shape the nose. Blend and curve all lines into a smooth, complete body shape. Erase any guidelines you no longer need.

Add eye patches

Flash fact: *Fewer than 1,000 giant pandas remain in the wild, in China's mountain bamboo forests. Giant pandas eat only bamboo—feeding up to 14 hours a day. As the bamboo forests disappear, so do these rare animals.*

4. Draw the eyes and nose in more detail. Then add the finishing touches by shading the panda's fur and adding the bamboo stalk—the giant panda's favorite food.

Northern Spotted Owl

The northern spotted owl has been involved in a controversy between timber companies and conservationists. Logging in old-growth forests, however, reduces this owl's natural habitat. Since 1990, certain areas have been set aside to save these birds from extinction.

Tip: It usually is easier to begin by sketching the largest shape first.

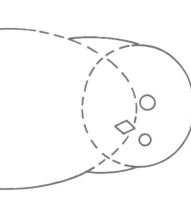

1. Begin with a large, lightly drawn oval for the owl's body. Add an overlapping circle for its head, then two short lines to connect the two shapes. Add the other basic guideline shapes for the eyes, beak, tree limb, claws, and tail feathers.

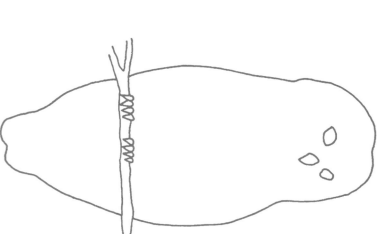

2. Combine and blend the shapes, erasing unneeded guidelines as you go along.

Flash fact: Only a few thousand pairs of northern spotted owls still live in the ancient forests along the Pacific coast of North America.

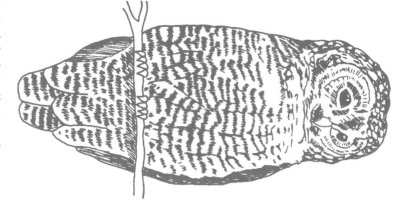

3. Add details to the eyes and face, then define the feathers. Complete your owl drawing by adding squiggly horizontal lines and shading.

Mediterranean Monk Seal

These shy seals breed inside caves on Mediterranean beaches. As more and more tourists visit the beaches, there are fewer spots for the seals. Pollution has also taken its toll.

1. Lightly draw a large oval for the seal's body and a smaller one for its head. Add the other basic guideline shapes for the eye, snout, and front and tail flippers. Connect the shapes as shown.

2. Blend the shapes into a sleek, smooth outline of the seal's body. Keep sketching and erasing until you are satisfied with your drawing at this step.

3. Complete the facial features and add lots of shading and texture to finish your monk seal drawing.

Flash fact: This seal has become the rarest mammal in Europe.

Eskimo Curlew

These birds migrate all the way from Alaska to Chile and back again each year. So many have been killed by hunters that, for a while, curlews were thought to be extinct.

Tip: Before you start, study the finished drawing in step 4. This will help you understand how the different shapes relate to one another.

1. Begin by lightly sketching a large oval guideline shape, creating the body. Then draw a small circle for the head and a smaller circle for the eye. Draw neck lines to connect the shapes, then add triangles for the tail feathers.

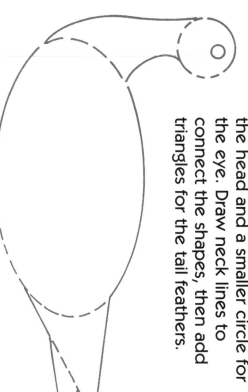

2. At the head, sketch a long, curved beak. Then sketch other guideline shapes, as shown, for the legs and feet. As you go along, erase any guidelines you no longer need.

4. Complete the eye, then add shading to the beak and legs. Define the short body feathers before shading them in.

Flash fact: Hunting of the Eskimo curlew has been banned, but it may have been too late to save the curlews. There may be only 100 left—if any.

3. Start blending the shapes into a smooth outline of the Eskimo curlew. Pay special attention to the legs and feet. When you are satisfied with the way your drawing looks, start adding the final details.

Komodo Dragon

The largest of the monitor lizards living today, the Komodo dragon is a 10-foot-long, 300-pound reptile that lives on the island of Komodo and on a few other small Indonesian islands.

1. Begin by drawing a large oval for the body and a smaller one for the head. Next, draw ovals and rectangles for the hind legs.

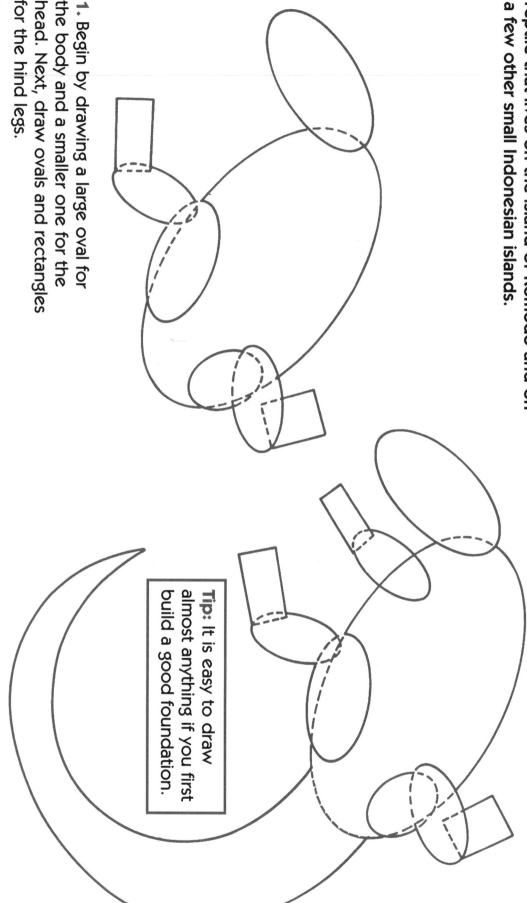

2. Next, add oval and rectangle guidelines for one foreleg. (The other is hidden from view.) Add two long, curved lines for the tail—as long as the head and body combined.

Tip: It is easy to draw almost anything if you first build a good foundation.

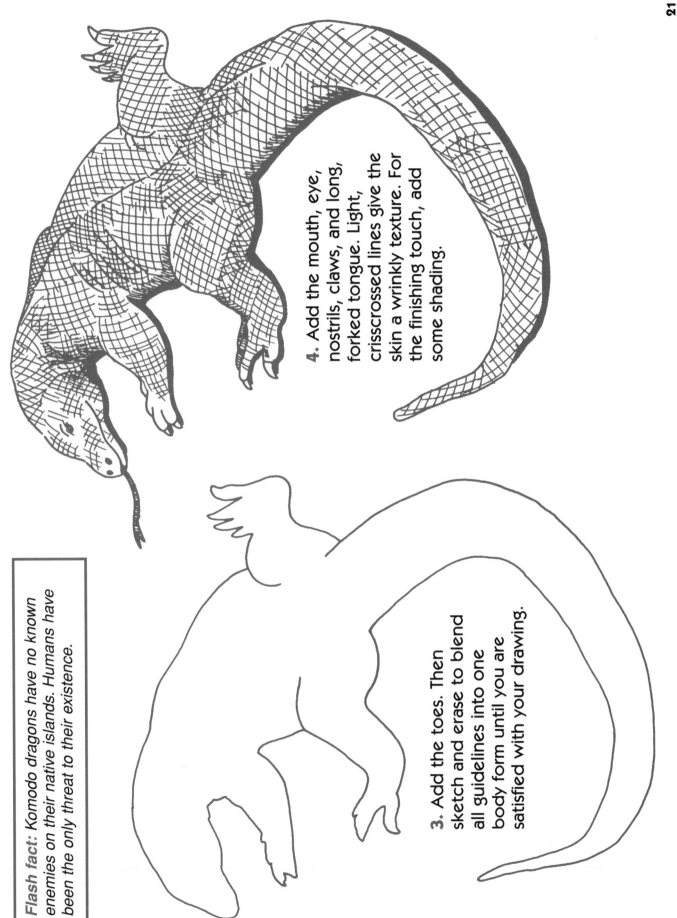

Flash fact: Komodo dragons have no known enemies on their native islands. Humans have been the only threat to their existence.

4. Add the mouth, eye, nostrils, claws, and long, forked tongue. Light, crisscrossed lines give the skin a wrinkly texture. For the finishing touch, add some shading.

3. Add the toes. Then sketch and erase to blend all guidelines into one body form until you are satisfied with your drawing.

Malayan Tapir

A tapir is something like a cross between a horse and a rhinoceros. As a baby, the Malayan tapir has a black-and-white spotted coat. As it grows older, its coat becomes half black (front end) and half white (back end).

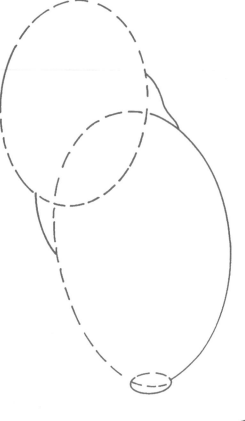

1. Begin by lightly sketching two large, overlapping ovals for the body, then connecting them as shown. Next, add a small oval for the tail.

2. Add the basic guideline shapes for the head, along with shapes for the ears, eye, and nose. Then sketch in the shapes for the legs and feet.

Tip: Dotted lines indicate guidelines that you will erase later, when you no longer need them.

3. Now blend the shapes together, erasing any guidelines you no longer need as you go along. Keep refining your picture until you are satisfied with the way it looks.

4. Carefully add lots of shading to give the tapir a more realistic, 3-D look.

Flash fact: The leaf-eating tapir is endangered due to overhunting, as well as the clearing of its forest habitat in Indonesia, Malaysia, Myanmar, and Thailand.

Red Wolf

Because wolves were greatly feared by farmers and ranchers, many of these striking animals were shot, trapped, or poisoned. Today, the natural habitats of red wolves—areas with heavy vegetative cover—are shrinking dramatically.

1. Sketch a basic oval shape for the body. Then draw a circle for the head and connect it to the body. Add triangles for the ears.

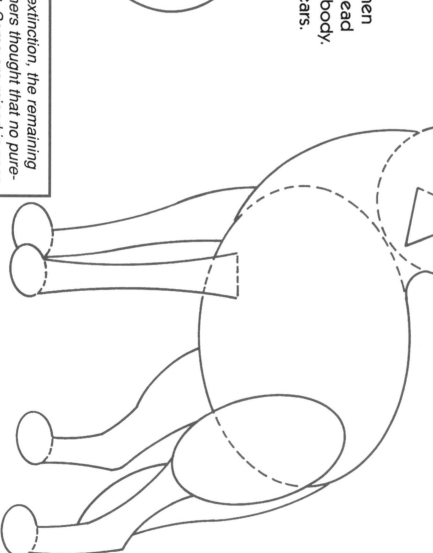

2. Add an oval for the hindquarters and guidelines for the legs and feet. Then sketch in the partially hidden tail, a triangle for the snout, and two tiny ovals for the eyes.

Flash fact: As hunters almost drove them toward extinction, the remaining red wolves bred with coyotes. For a while, researchers thought that no pure-bred red wolves were left. However, some still exist. Some are raised in zoos. Others are being released into protected preserves.

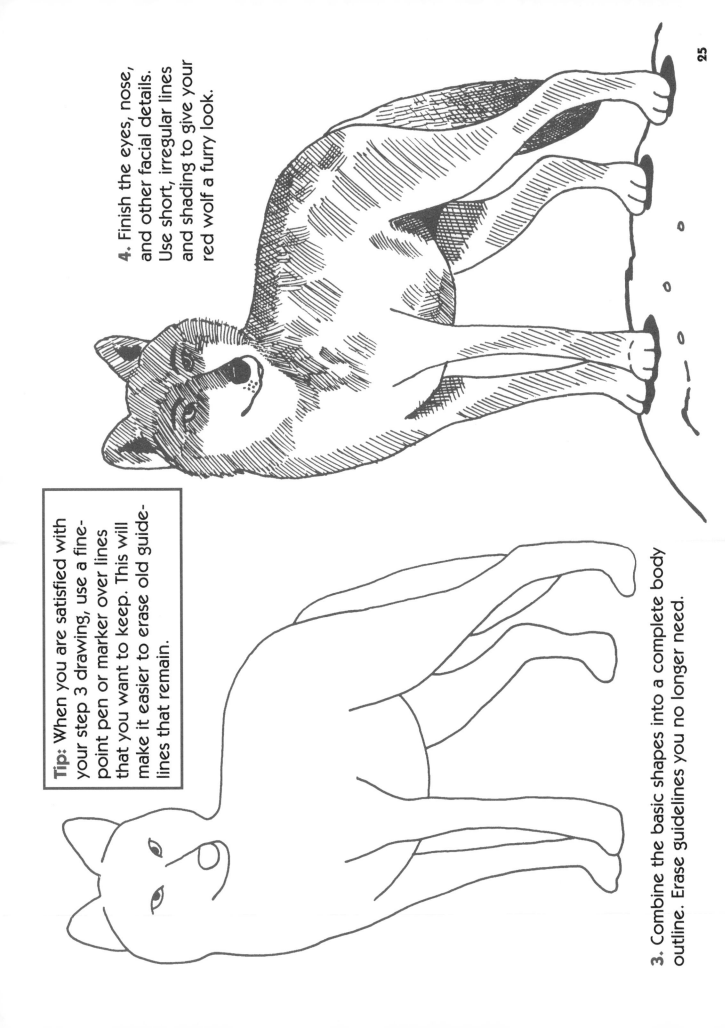

4. Finish the eyes, nose, and other facial details. Use short, irregular lines and shading to give your red wolf a furry look.

Tip: When you are satisfied with your step 3 drawing, use a fine-point pen or marker over lines that you want to keep. This will make it easier to erase old guidelines that remain.

3. Combine the basic shapes into a complete body outline. Erase guidelines you no longer need.

Mountain Gorilla

A small area in Africa is the last home of these shy and gentle primates. The rapid destruction of the forests in which they live forces mountain gorillas to move farther and farther into remote areas.

1. Start by drawing three ovals as guides for the head, shoulder area, and hindquarters. Connect them to each other. Then add the arms and hands.

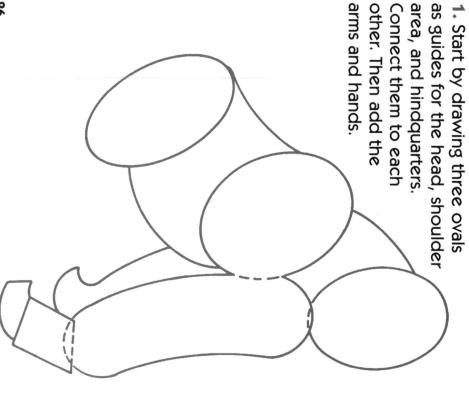

Tip: No one gets it right the first time! Always use soft, light pencil strokes, especially in the early steps. Being able to erase and redraw is a very important part of the process.

2. Next, add ovals for the legs and feet, as shown.

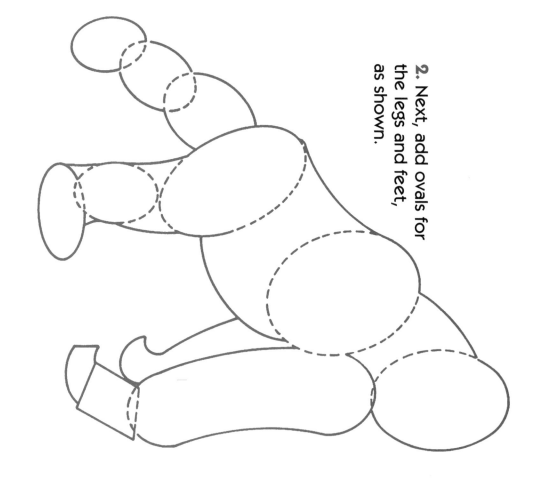

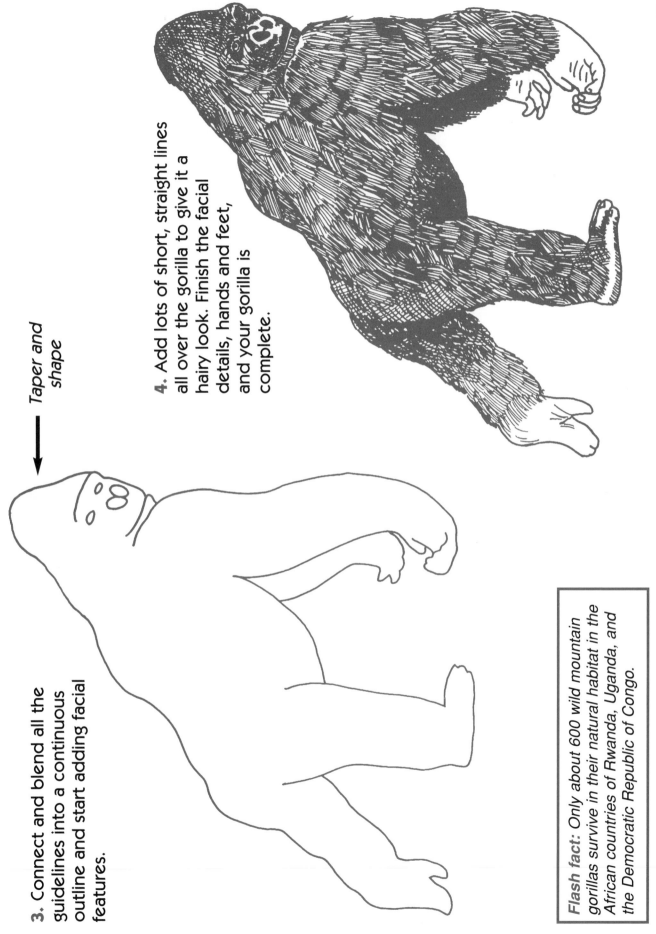

3. Connect and blend all the guidelines into a continuous outline and start adding facial features.

Taper and shape

4. Add lots of short, straight lines all over the gorilla to give it a hairy look. Finish the facial details, hands and feet, and your gorilla is complete.

Flash fact: Only about 600 wild mountain gorillas survive in their natural habitat in the African countries of Rwanda, Uganda, and the Democratic Republic of Congo.

Black-footed Ferret

This very rare ferret's existence has long been tied to the survival of prairie dogs, on which they prey. Once widespread throughout the American Great Plains, prairie dog "towns" have been greatly reduced by the spread of agriculture, ranching, and new housing.

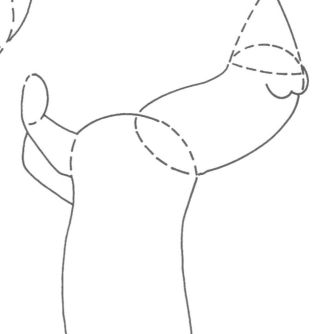

Tip: Focus on one part of the body at a time. Keep erasing and sketching until you are satisfied with that area before moving on to another.

1. Start with a lightly drawn, long oval shape for the body. Add a smaller overlapping oval for the hindquarters.

2. Sketch a triangular shape for the head, then draw neck lines to connect it to the body. Next, add shapes for the four short legs and paws, as shown, and the curly tail.

3. Start erasing any guidelines that are no longer needed as you combine the shapes together.

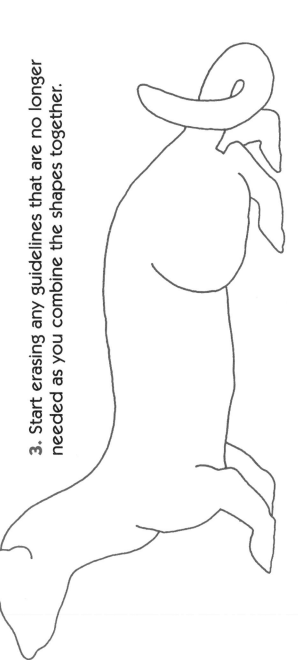

4. Finish the facial features and add details and shading to complete your drawing. Note the dark "mask" on the face of the black-footed ferret.

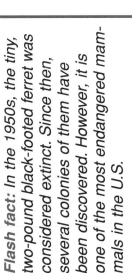

Flash fact: In the 1950s, the tiny, two-pound black-footed ferret was considered extinct. Since then, several colonies of them have been discovered. However, it is one of the most endangered mammals in the U.S.

Fijian Banded Iguana

This rare, long-toed lizard likes to hang out in trees. But trees are becoming scarce on the Pacific islands where it lives, threatening this iguana's survival.

1. First, draw a long, free-form oval for the iguana's body. Next, add two overlapping ovals for the head. Remember to keep all your guideline shapes lightly drawn, so you can revise them later.

2. Sketch two very long lines to create the curvy tail. Then add the other basic shapes for the legs, feet, and long claws.

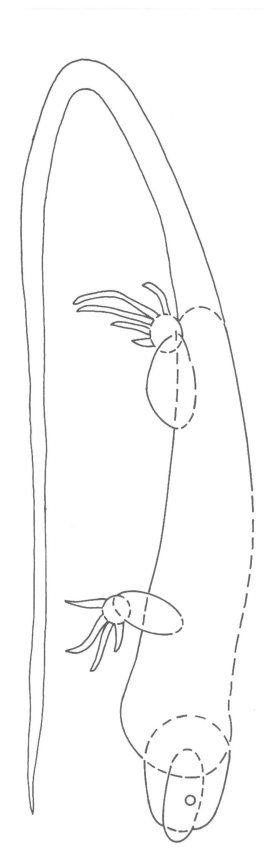

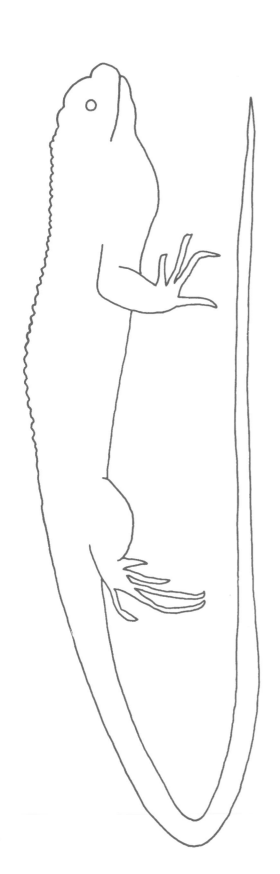

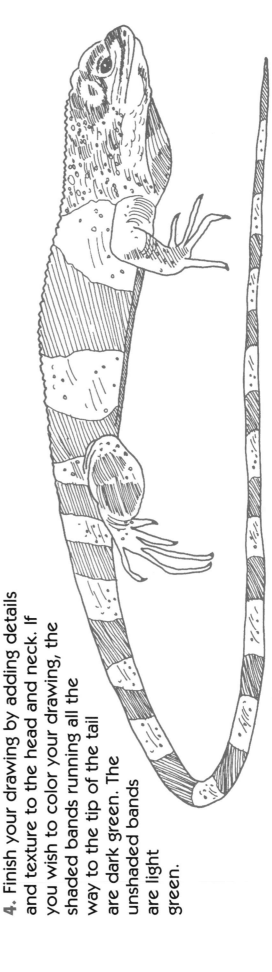

3. Combine all the shapes to form a simple line drawing. Note the squiggly line on the iguana's back.

4. Finish your drawing by adding details and texture to the head and neck. If you wish to color your drawing, the shaded bands running all the way to the tip of the tail are dark green. The unshaded bands are light green.

Flash fact: One of the iguana's worst enemies is the mongoose, which eats its eggs and young.

Scimitar-horned Oryx

This rarest of antelopes is found in semidesert areas of the Sahara. By the mid-1980s, due to excessive hunting, this magnificent animal was on the brink of extinction. Its close relative, the Arabian oryx, is also an endangered species.

1. Begin this oryx with two ovals—one for the shoulder area and one for the hindquarters. The connecting lines between the two ovals form the back and belly. Next, draw ovals and a circle for the head. Add connecting lines to form the animal's neck.

Connect

Connect

2. Add more ovals for the top part of the legs, then connect them to the triangular hooves. Add simple shapes to start the long, curved horns and a tail.

Triangles

Taper

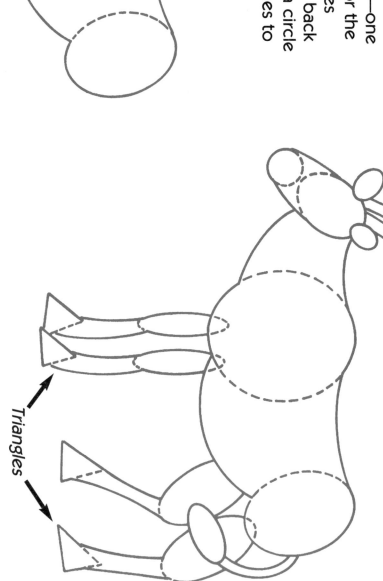

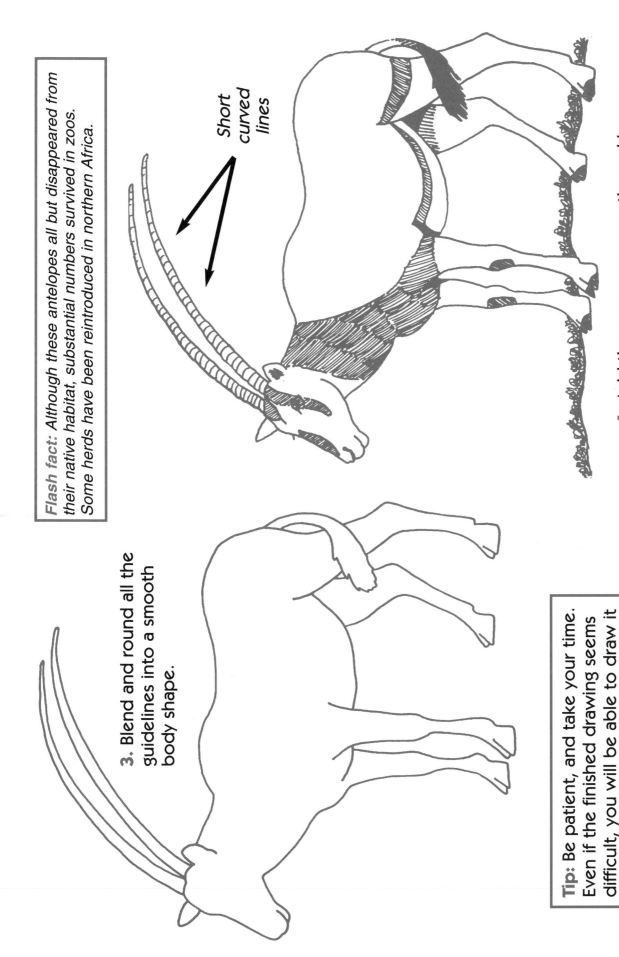

Flash fact: Although these antelopes all but disappeared from their native habitat, substantial numbers survived in zoos. Some herds have been reintroduced in northern Africa.

Short curved lines

3. Blend and round all the guidelines into a smooth body shape.

4. Add the eye, nose, mouth, and hooves. Complete the oryx by adding texture to the horns, and shading the body as shown.

Tip: Be patient, and take your time. Even if the finished drawing seems difficult, you will be able to draw it if you follow along, step by step.

Helmeted Hornbill

This bird of southeast Asia is being threatened by loss of habitat due to tree felling and poachers.

Tip: It usually is easier to begin by sketching the largest shape first.

1. Start by drawing a free-form oval for this bird's body, then a smaller one for its head. Connect the shapes with a curved neckline. Add the eye, the large triangular beak, and the crest on top of the beak.

2. Sketch in two long, overlapping ovals for the tail feathers. Add the additional basic shapes as shown. Always draw your guide-lines lightly in steps 1 and 2—it will be easier to erase them later.

4. Finish drawing the eye and crested beak. Then carefully add the body feathers—first, sketch overlapping ovals, then shade them in. Don't forget to draw a branch for the helmeted hornbill to perch on.

Flash fact: The solid lump on the hornbill's beak is made of substance very like ivory. Highly prized, it was carved for jewelry and religious items.

3. Blend the lines and shapes together, erasing unnecessary guidelines. Note that, due to the feathers, the outline is not completely smooth.

Leatherback Sea Turtle

Overhunting and pollution have combined to reduce most sea turtle species to an endangered state. The leatherback is by far the largest of all turtles, on land or at sea. An adult can weigh 1,500 pounds and measure 8 feet in length.

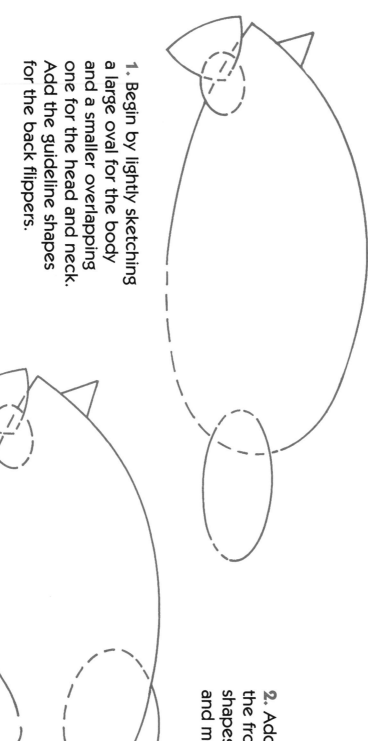

1. Begin by lightly sketching a large oval for the body and a smaller overlapping one for the head and neck. Add the guideline shapes for the back flippers.

2. Add two more ovals for the front flippers, then basic shapes for the eye, beak, and mouth, as shown.

3. Blend all the shapes into a smooth, turtle-body shape. Continue to erase guidelines you no longer need as you refine your drawing. Note the way the front of the shell curves.

Tip: Keep drawing and erasing until your outline is just right.

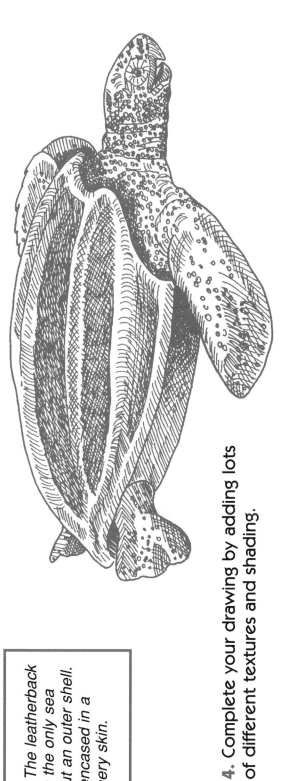

Flash fact: The leatherback sea turtle is the only sea turtle without an outer shell. Its shell is encased in a tough, leathery skin.

4. Complete your drawing by adding lots of different textures and shading.

Aye-aye

The aye-aye and other lemurs are found only on the island of Madagascar. This pop-eyed creature has a super-long middle finger, which it uses to pull insects out of tree bark.

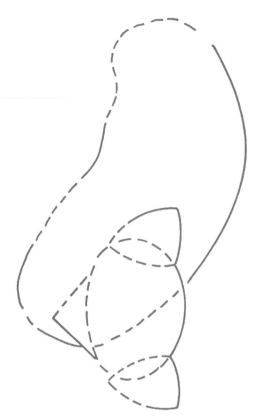

1. Draw the large basic guideline shape for the body. Then add an overlapping oval for the head and triangles for the ears and snout.

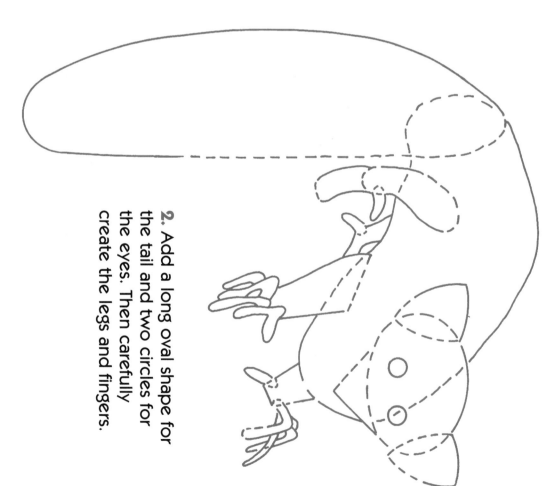

2. Add a long oval shape for the tail and two circles for the eyes. Then carefully create the legs and fingers.

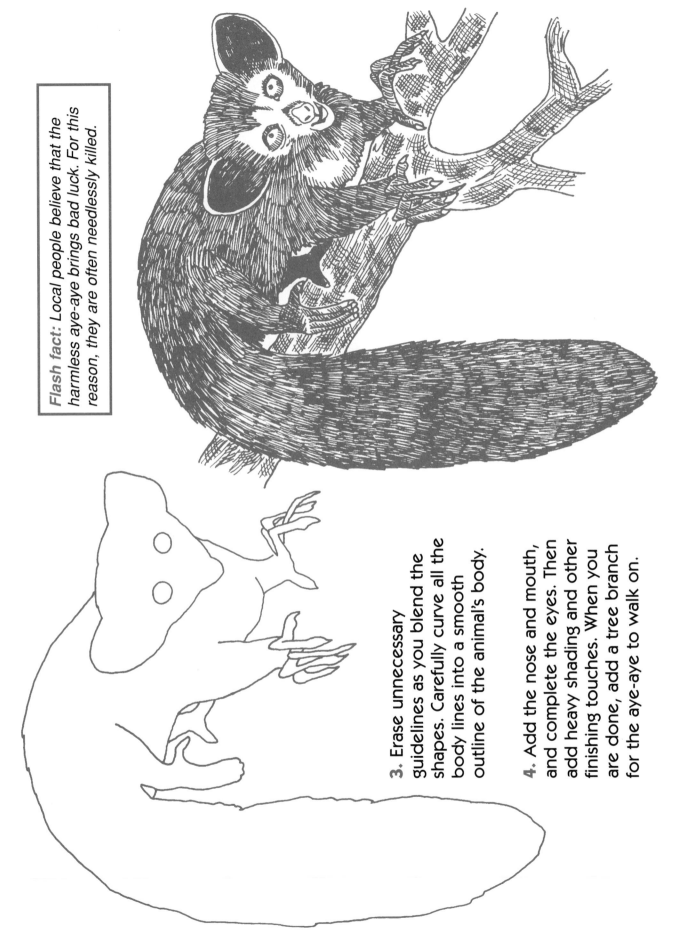

Flash fact: Local people believe that the harmless aye-aye brings bad luck. For this reason, they are often needlessly killed.

3. Erase unnecessary guidelines as you blend the shapes. Carefully curve all the body lines into a smooth outline of the animal's body.

4. Add the nose and mouth, and complete the eyes. Then add heavy shading and other finishing touches. When you are done, add a tree branch for the aye-aye to walk on.

Indri

Indris belong to the lemur family. They live only in remote areas of the island of Madagascar, on preserves set up to protect them.

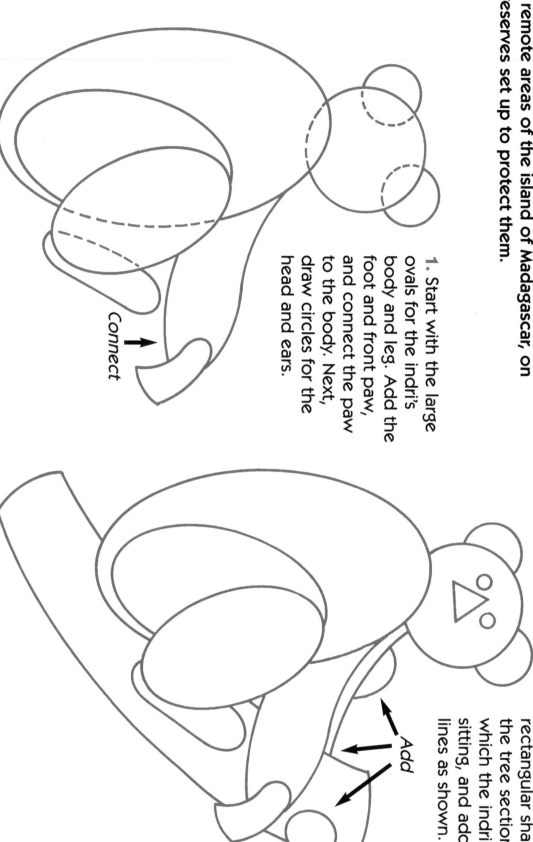

Connect

1. Start with the large ovals for the indri's body and leg. Add the foot and front paw, and connect the paw to the body. Next, draw circles for the head and ears.

Add

2. Draw a triangle for the nose and two small circles for the eyes. Add a long, rectangular shape for the tree section on which the indri is sitting, and additional lines as shown.

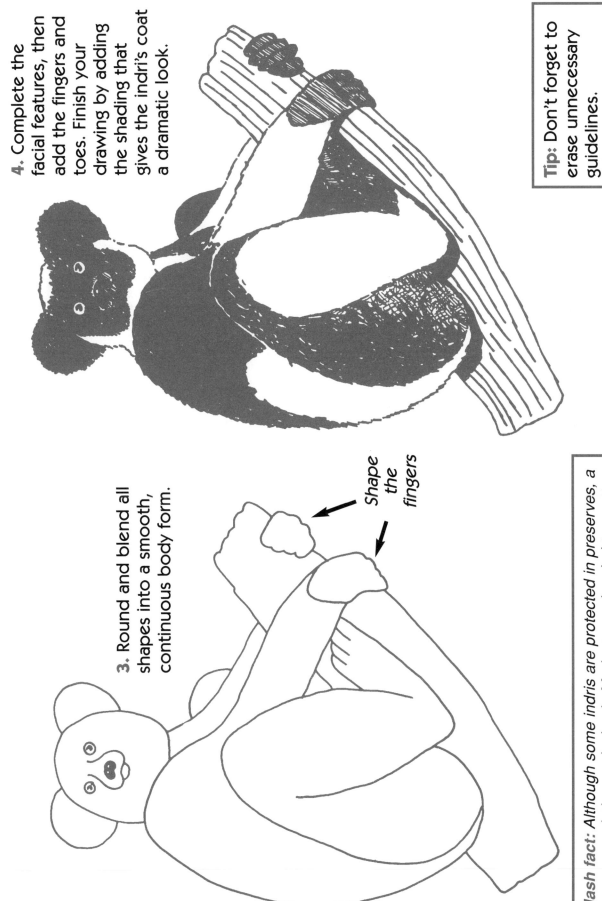

4. Complete the facial features, then add the fingers and toes. Finish your drawing by adding the shading that gives the indri's coat a dramatic look.

3. Round and blend all shapes into a smooth, continuous body form.

Shape the fingers

Tip: Don't forget to erase unnecessary guidelines.

Flash fact: Although some indris are protected in preserves, a human population explosion in Madagascar has led to greater loss of the indri's true home, the forest.

Indigo Macaw

So many South American macaws have been trapped and sold as pets that they have completely disappeared from many areas. At a length of up to three feet, this purplish-blue bird is the longest of all parrots. It also is known as Lear's macaw.

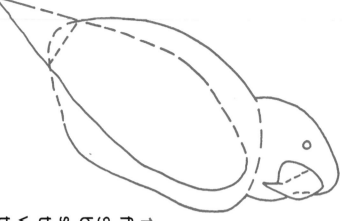

Tip: Don't be afraid to erase and redraw. No one gets it right the first time.

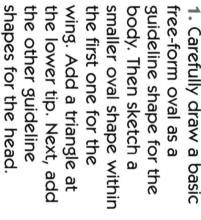

1. Carefully draw a basic free-form oval as a guideline shape for the body. Then sketch a smaller oval shape within the first one for the wing. Add a triangle at the lower tip. Next, add the other guideline shapes for the head.

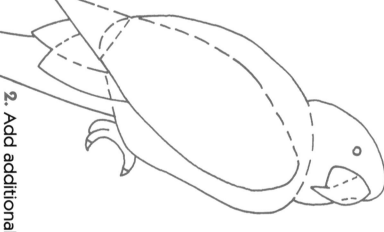

2. Add additional triangular shapes for the tail feathers, as shown. Next, sketch in curved lines for the claws. Erase any unnecessary guide-lines as you begin to refine your drawing.

4. Define the individual feathers before shading them in. Add details, texture, and more shading to give your drawing a realistic look. Don't forget to draw a limb for the macaw's perch.

3. Blend and smooth all the shapes together into a complete body outline.

Jaguar

Long hunted for its beautiful coat, the jaguar is now a protected species. Due to the ever-shrinking forests of Central and South America, the number of jaguars is decreasing with each passing year.

1. Begin with a series of lightly drawn, interconnecting ovals, as shown.

Remember: Keep all lines lightly drawn until the final step.

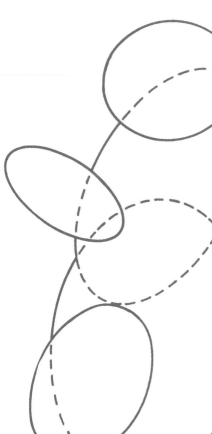

2. Add guideline shapes for the ears, eyes, nose, and mouth. Then draw additional ovals for the legs and paws, and long, curved lines for the tail.

Unlike other spotted cats, the jaguar's spots are enclosed by a circular pattern.

Flash fact: As South American forests in Brazil and Peru are chopped down, the jaguar has no place to go. Hunters also seek the large cat's beautiful skin. Reserves and antihunting laws now protect these sleek animals.

Indent

Indent

3. Connect and blend all the shapes. Erase the guidelines you no longer need.

4. For the final step, add in all the details. Draw the jaguar's unique coat pattern and add some background scenery. Use your imagination to create a jungle scene.

Resplendent Quetzal

This beautiful Central American bird has a red breast and green tail feathers that extend up to 30 inches. However, this beauty makes people want to keep them as pets, so they are fast disappearing from the wild.

Tip: Always draw your guidelines lightly in steps 1 and 2, so they will be easier to erase later on.

1. Begin with an oval for the body and an overlapping circle for the head. Add the other guideline shapes, as shown, for the wing, foot, and upper tail feathers.

2. Add this long, graceful shape for the resplendent quetzal's magnificent tail feathers.

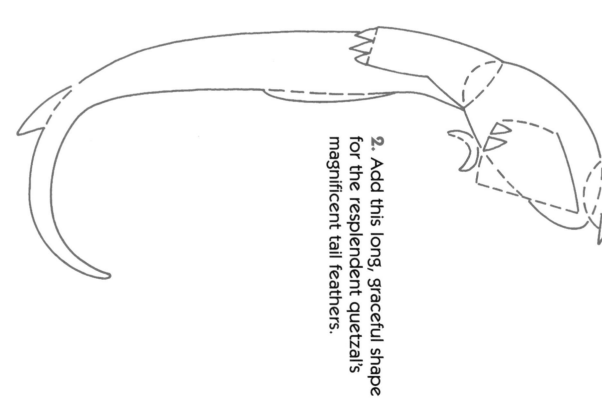

4. Complete the eye and the head feathers. Then draw the body and tail feathers, adding shading and texture. When you are done, add a branch for the resplendent quetzal's perch.

Flash fact: Much of the mountain forest in which the resplendent quetzal lives is being cleared to make way for farming.

3. Blend the shapes into a more finished body outline, erasing guidelines and defining some of the feathers.

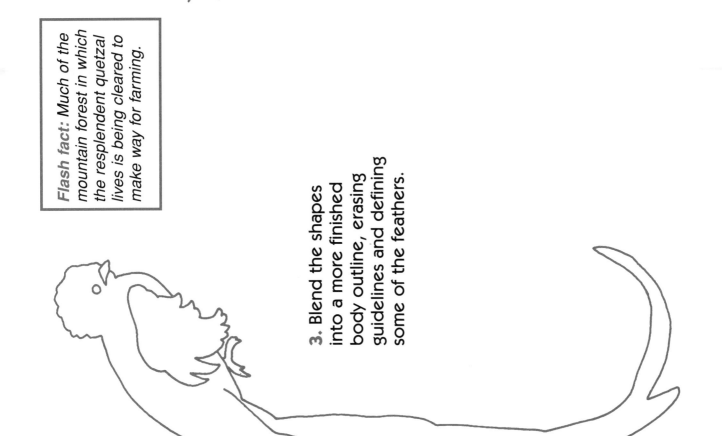

Spectacled Bear

This bear gets its name from the white rings around its eyes. It lives in trees, sleeping by day and hunting for fruit at night. It is becoming increasingly scarce as its natural habitat is cleared for farmland.

Remember: It usually is easier to begin by sketching the largest shape first.

1. Begin with a large, slightly curving rectangular shape for the bear's body. Add an overlapping circle for its head, and the other basic guideline shapes, as shown.

2. Add these guideline shapes for the arms, paws, legs, and feet. Remember to keep your lines lightly drawn.

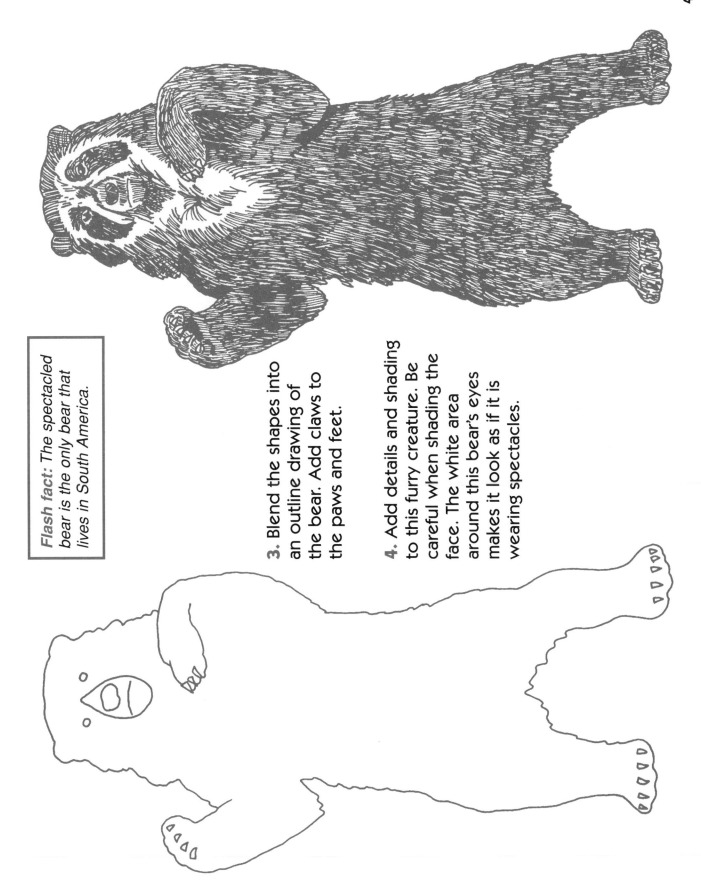

Flash fact: The spectacled bear is the only bear that lives in South America.

3. Blend the shapes into an outline drawing of the bear. Add claws to the paws and feet.

4. Add details and shading to this furry creature. Be careful when shading the face. The white area around this bear's eyes makes it look as if it is wearing spectacles.

Black Rhinoceros

The black rhinoceros can be found in the grassland, bush, and the forest areas of Africa.

Remember: Dotted lines indicate guidelines that you will erase when you no longer need them.

1. Begin with lightly drawn ovals for the body, head, and ears. Add triangles for the horns.

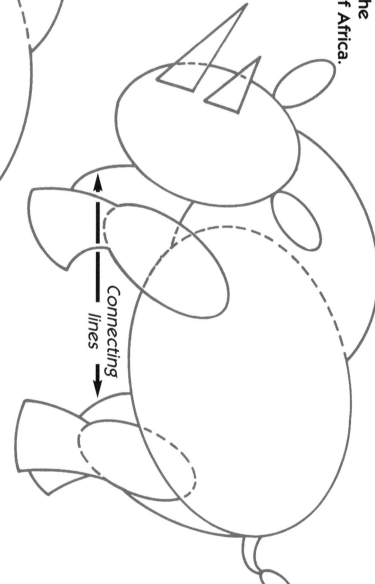

Connecting lines

2. Draw guideline shapes to start the legs and tail, then add connecting lines, as shown.

50

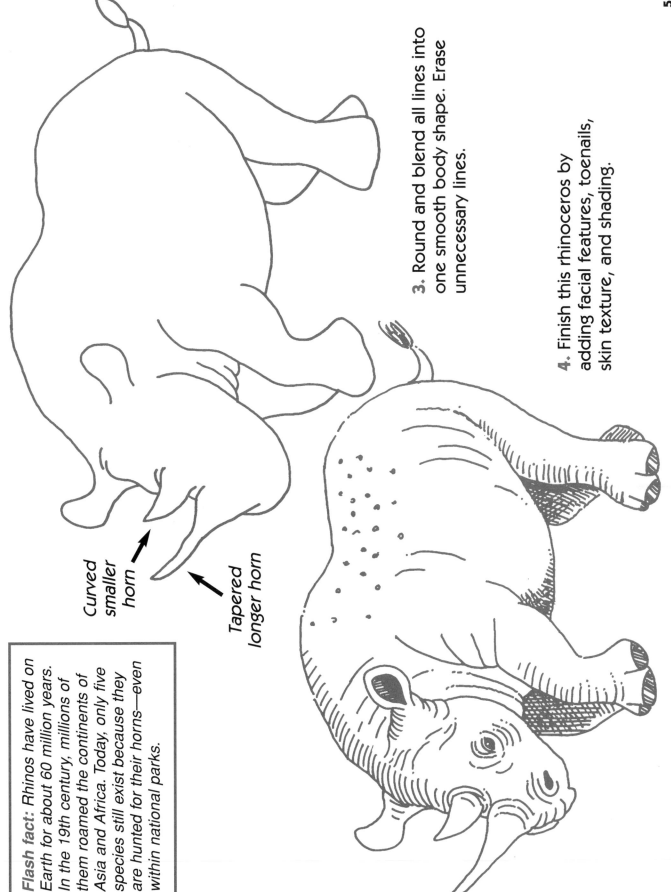

Flash fact: Rhinos have lived on Earth for about 60 million years. In the 19th century, millions of them roamed the continents of Asia and Africa. Today, only five species still exist because they are hunted for their horns—even within national parks.

Curved smaller horn

Tapered longer horn

3. Round and blend all lines into one smooth body shape. Erase unnecessary lines.

4. Finish this rhinoceros by adding facial features, toenails, skin texture, and shading.

Queen Alexandra's Birdwing

Found only in New Guinea, this is the biggest butterfly in the world. It has been hunted because of its great value to collectors. Some people are now planning to breed the Queen Alexandra's birdwing on ranches.

1. Start this beautiful butterfly by lightly sketching two slender overlapping oval guideline shapes for the body. Add two tiny circles for the eyes, then two graceful lines for the antennae.

2. Lightly sketch four over-lapping ovals for the wings.

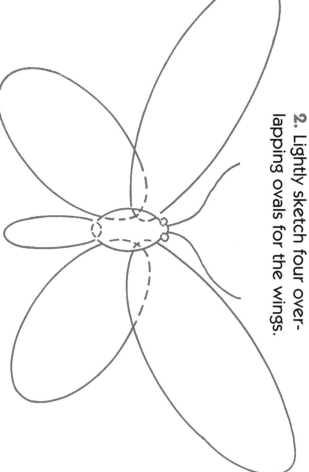

Tip: Take your time, especially with the first two steps. If you get them right, the rest of your drawing will be easier to do.

Flash fact: This butterfly's wingspan is between 6 and 10 inches. A real one would barely fit on this page.

3. Blend the guideline shapes into a clean outline of the butterfly. Don't be afraid to erase and redraw any-thing that you are not satisfied with.

4. Add lots of lines, details, and shading as shown. When your drawing is complete, add a few flowers around the butterfly to make it feel at home.

Przewalski's Horse

This endangered animal was named after a Russian explorer who discovered it in the late 1870s. Once abundant throughout central Asia, this wild horse has been hunted by humans to near extinction.

Tip: This drawing may look difficult, but if you take your time and work carefully, step by step, you will find that you can do it.

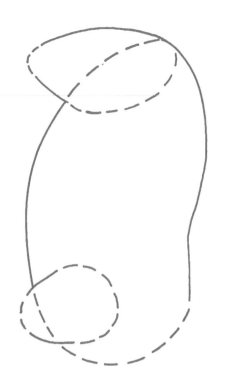

1. Start with a thick, free-form oval for the body. Add two smaller overlapping ones for the shoulder and rump.

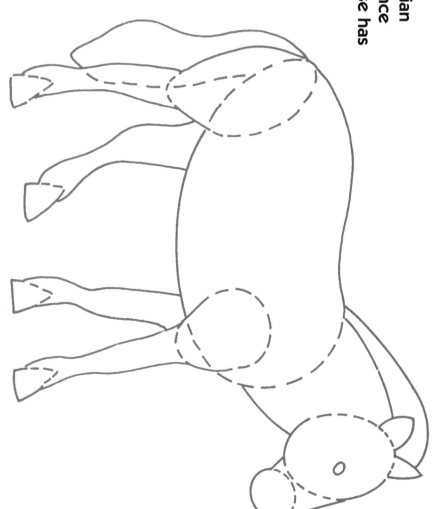

2. Add basic guideline shapes for the legs and hooves, as shown. Then draw an oval for the head and a circle for the nose, and connect the two shapes. Add the ears, then connect the head to the body. Finally, add a guideline for the horse's mane.

3. Blend the shapes into a clean, smooth outline sketch, erasing any guidelines you no longer need.

Flash fact: Within a few hours after birth, a wild colt can run fast enough to keep up with the herd.

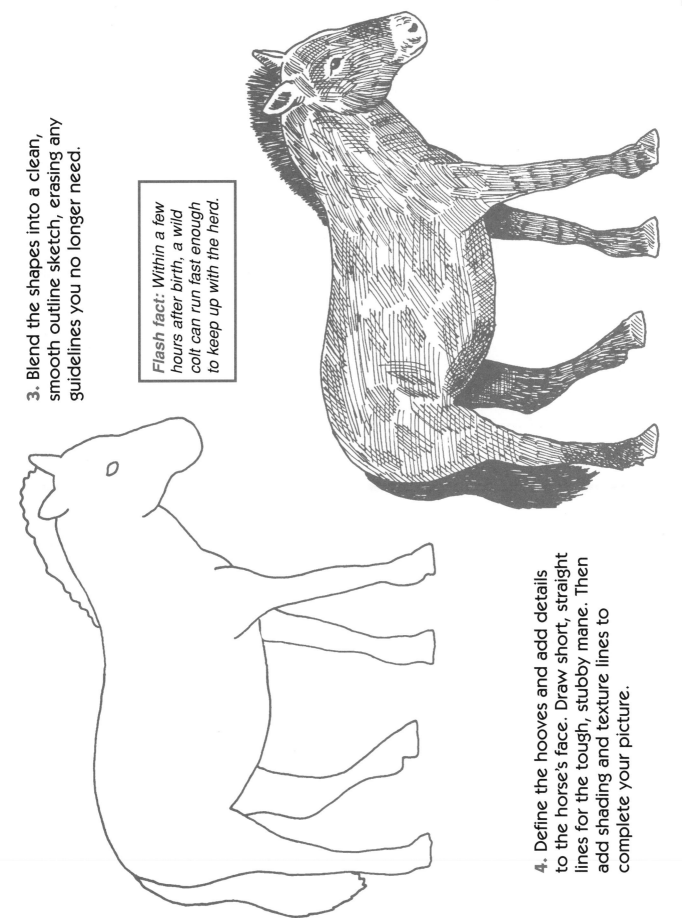

4. Define the hooves and add details to the horse's face. Draw short, straight lines for the tough, stubby mane. Then add shading and texture lines to complete your picture.

Shortnose Sturgeon

Sturgeons live in the open sea most of the time. They swim inland through rivers and streams only to lay their eggs. With more and more dams being built, it is harder each year for the fish to get through.

1. Sketch a very long narrow oval, rounder at the front end and pointier at the back end, for the body. Add a guideline shape for the head and pointy snout, and triangular shapes for the tail.

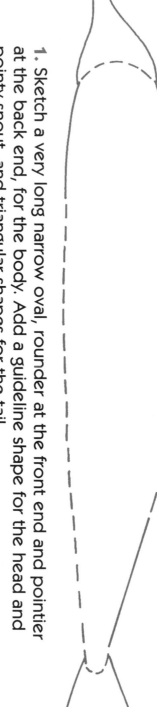

2. Add the eye and fins, then sketch a row of small diamond shapes along the length of the sturgeon's body.

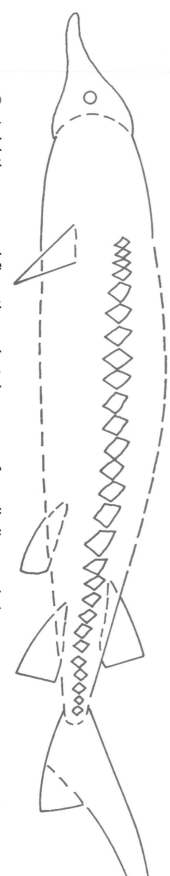

Flash fact: Sturgeons have been overhunted for food. In addition, females contain one of the world's expensive delicacies—her eggs, known as caviar.

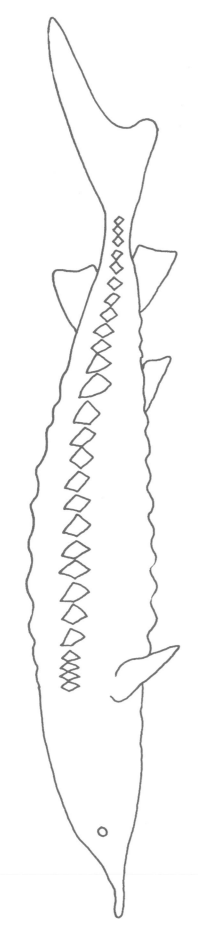

3. Erase and sketch to blend the shapes, forming a simple line drawing. Note that the outlines of the back and belly are bumpy, not straight.

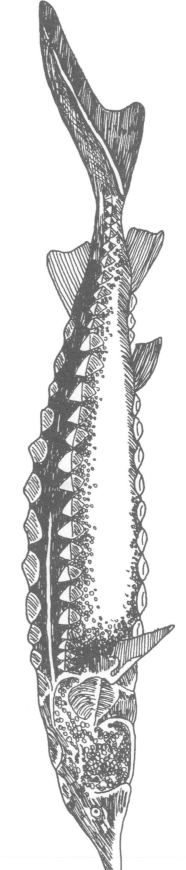

4. Lots of different textures and shading are required to complete this picture. First, add the details. Then work on the shading until your picture is finished.

Giant Otter

Giant otters live in family groups on the banks of several rivers in South America. They can measure more than 6 feet in length and weigh up to 75 pounds. This increasingly rare otter is threatened by overhunting and loss of habitat.

Flash fact: Otters make many different sounds. They chirp, chatter, bark, and growl.

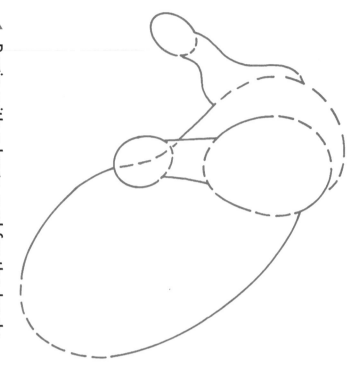

1. Begin with a large oval for the body. Draw a smaller oval for the shoulder and another for the left paw, then add lines to connect them. Then draw the right paw and connect it to the body.

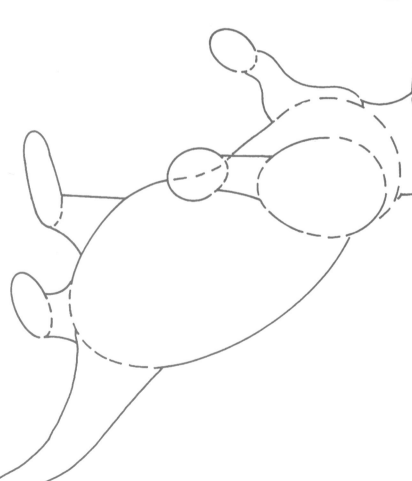

2. Draw an oval guideline for the otter's head, then connect it to the body. Add the nose, eye, and ear. Next, add guideline shapes for the rear legs and paws, and the long, curved tail.

4. Draw the mouth and refine the facial features. Then add shading, details, and the finishing touches, such as whiskers, to give your giant otter drawing a realistic look.

Tip: Make sure that you are satisfied with the way your drawing looks before going on to step 4.

3. Blend the lines and shapes, erasing guidelines as you go along. The basic otter body shape is now complete.

Ivory-billed Woodpecker

This black and white woodpecker eats beetle grubs found only in the dead wood of very old trees. Logging has destroyed many first-growth forests, and the woodpecker's food along with them.

1. Start by drawing a large oval—pointed at the bottom—for the body. Then draw a similar oval inside the first one, for the wing. (Note how the top of the wing's oval is pointed in a different direction from the top of the body's oval.) Sketch the simple shapes for the foot.

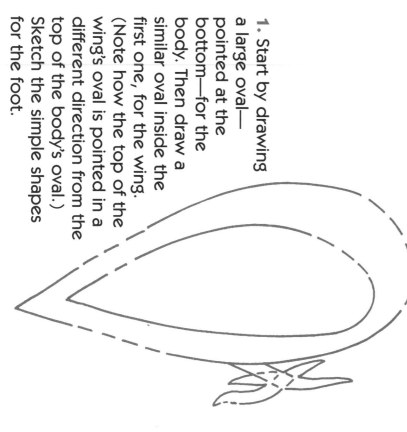

2. Add an oval for the head and connect it to the body. Then lightly sketch the other basic shapes shown, for the eye, crest, beak, and tail feathers.

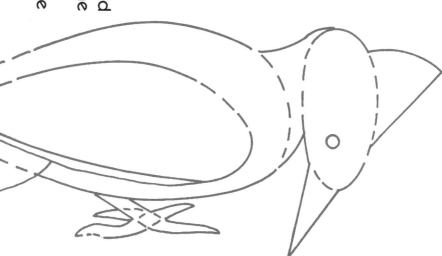

Remember: Even a complicated drawing will be easier to do if you focus on one area at a time and look for basic shapes.

4. Define the tail wing feathers before shading them in. Then add lots of details and texture. Create the (red) crest on the bird's head with short, slightly bent lines. Finally, add a tree for the woodpecker to peck into.

3. Blend the shapes together into a smooth woodpecker body outline.

Rodrigues Flying Fox

This rare, fruit-eating bat lives on Rodrigues, an island in the Indian Ocean that is part of the African nation of Mauritius.

Remember: It usually helps to start by drawing the largest shape first.

1. Begin by sketching a large oval for the body. Add two small triangles for the ears and an overlapping free-form oval for the head. Then sketch two small circles for the eyes and small triangle for the nose.

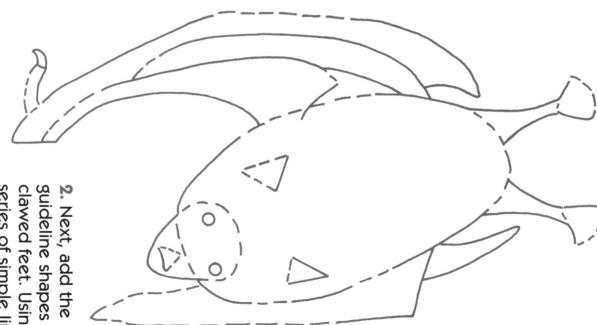

2. Next, add the legs and guideline shapes for the clawed feet. Using a series of simple lines and shapes, add the wings.

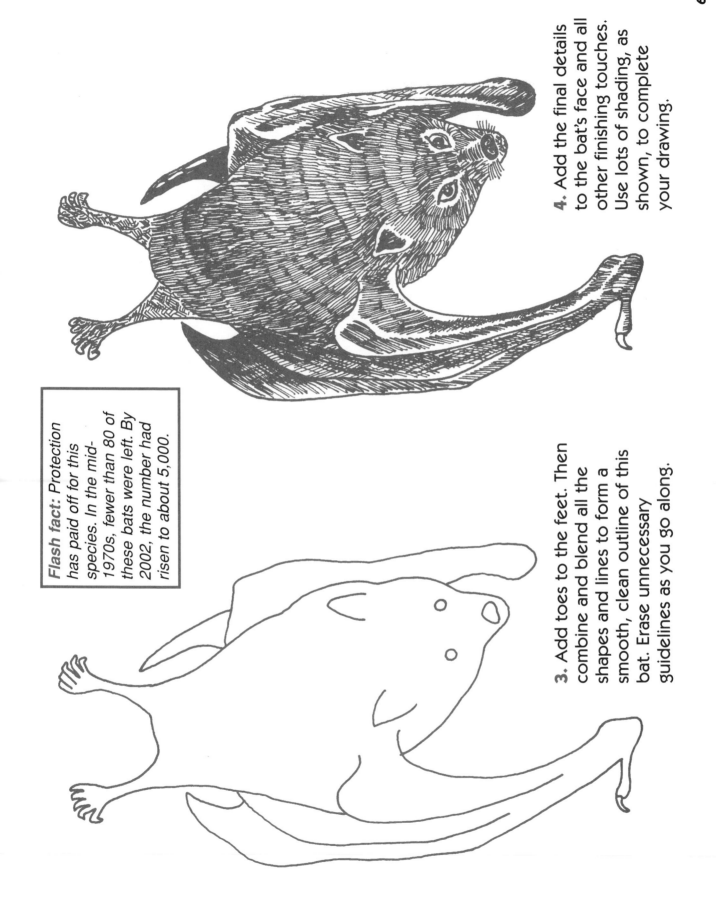

4. Add the final details to the bat's face and all other finishing touches. Use lots of shading, as shown, to complete your drawing.

Flash fact: Protection has paid off for this species. In the mid-1970s, fewer than 80 of these bats were left. By 2002, the number had risen to about 5,000.

3. Add toes to the feet. Then combine and blend all the shapes and lines to form a smooth, clean outline of this bat. Erase unnecessary guidelines as you go along.

Addax

This North African antelope has beautiful, curved horns that protect it from its natural enemies—but not from hunters, who seek the horns as trophies.

Remember: All lines in steps 1 and 2 should be lightly drawn.

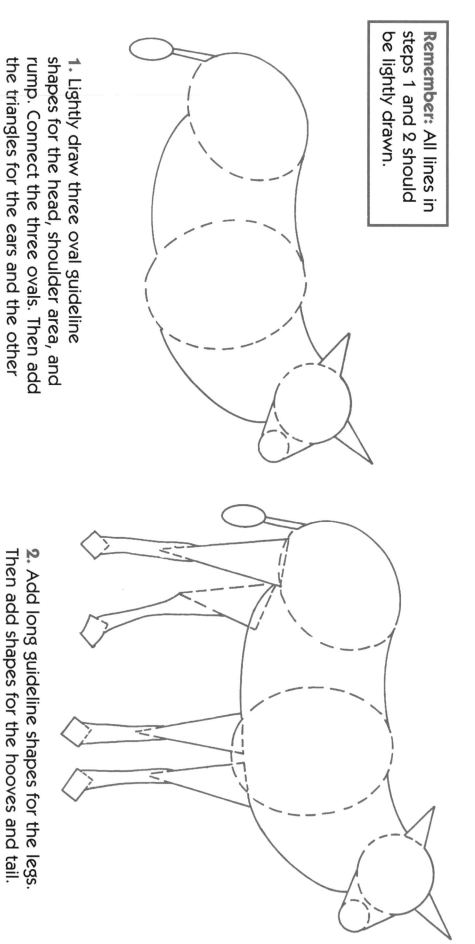

1. Lightly draw three oval guideline shapes for the head, shoulder area, and rump. Connect the three ovals. Then add the triangles for the ears and the other basic shapes for the snout and tail.

2. Add long guideline shapes for the legs. Then add shapes for the hooves and tail.

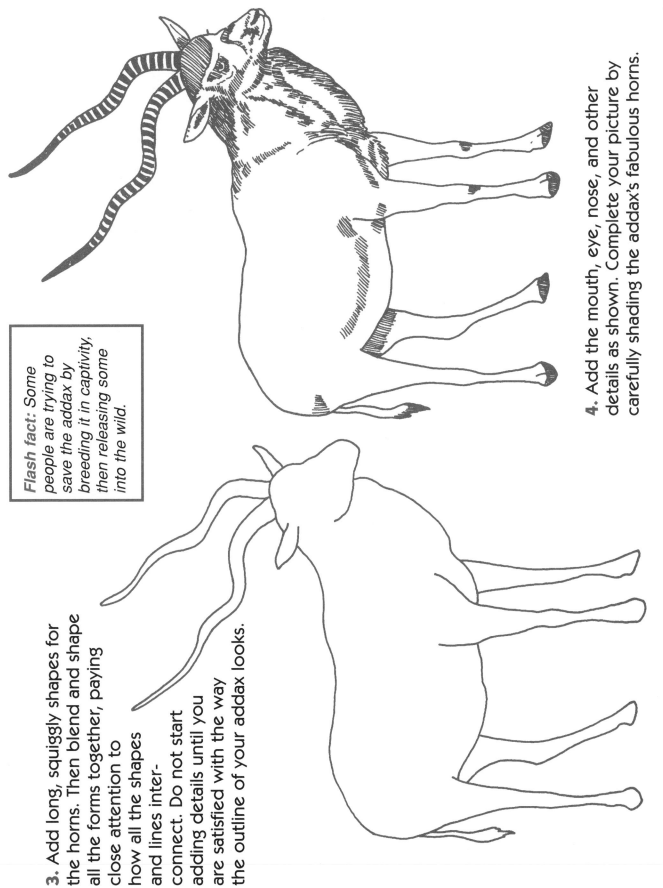

Flash fact: Some people are trying to save the addax by breeding it in captivity, then releasing some into the wild.

3. Add long, squiggly shapes for the horns. Then blend and shape all the forms together, paying close attention to how all the shapes and lines interconnect. Do not start adding details until you are satisfied with the way the outline of your addax looks.

4. Add the mouth, eye, nose, and other details as shown. Complete your picture by carefully shading the addax's fabulous horns.

Indian Python

The Indian python can grow to more than 20 feet. Though its coils are powerful enough to squeeze a leopard to death, it prefers small prey, such as rats. This python has suffered from loss of its habitat, being hunted for its beautiful skin, and being captured for the pet trade.

Tip: There are many overlapping shapes to draw in the first two steps, so proceed lightly and carefully. Look for the simple shapes inside the more complicated ones.

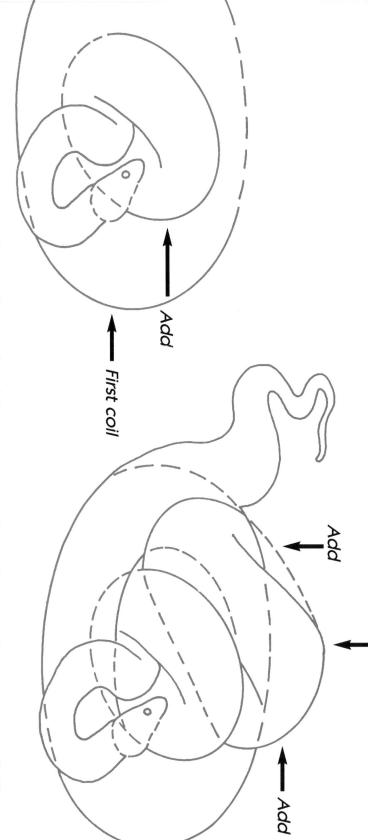

First coil

Add

Second coil

Add

Add

1. Lightly draw a large oval shape. Add a smaller oval inside the first one. This part of the python's body is coiled around its prey. Next, draw the python's head. Then add two curved lines to connect the head to the center of the smaller oval.

2. Next, draw the long curved tail. Then add another oval shape that overlaps your first two. This will form the second coil. This step is complicated, so take your time.

3. Erase and sketch to blend and shape all the body lines. Carefully erase the guidelines you no longer need.

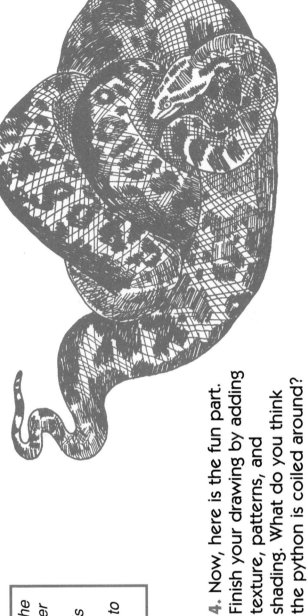

4. Now, here is the fun part. Finish your drawing by adding texture, patterns, and shading. What do you think the python is coiled around?

Flash fact: Unlike most snakes, the female Indian python stays with her eggs and helps them hatch by keeping them warm. She does this by coiling and twitching her body around the eggs. She may lay up to 60 eggs at a time.

Proboscis Monkey

This strange-looking monkey has a large, fleshy nose. It lives in riverside swamps and forests on the island of Borneo. Much of its habitat has been cleared to make way for human settlement.

1. Being with a large, free-form oval shape as a guideline for the body. Then sketch a smaller one for the head. Within the head oval, draw two smaller ones for the face and nose. Next, add overlapping oval guidelines for the upper arms and legs.

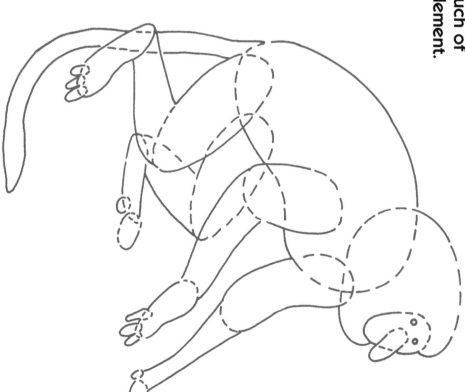

2. Add the eyes, then complete the guideline shapes for the rest of the arms, hands, legs, and feet.

Remember: Do not begin adding the finishing touches until you are completely satisfied with the way your drawing looks.

4. Complete the facial features. Then add shading and other details to the mane and body. This monkey has long hair on its neck and chest and shorter hair on the rest of its body. Don't forget to add a little shading to that long nose!

3. Carefully erase any guidelines that you no longer need as you blend and refine all shapes and lines.

Flash fact: Only the male proboscis monkey has the long nose. Sometimes, he has to push its nose out of the way to eat!

Hawksbill Sea Turtle

Most marine turtles are at risk due to several reasons. They all lay their eggs on beaches, many of which are no longer deserted. In some areas of the world, they are hunted for their meat. Pollution has also taken its toll.

1. Sketch a large oval that is pointed on one end for the body. Then sketch a small oval for the head, adding the eye and beak. Add the basic guideline shapes for back flippers.

2. Add oval shapes and connector lines for the front flippers, as shown.

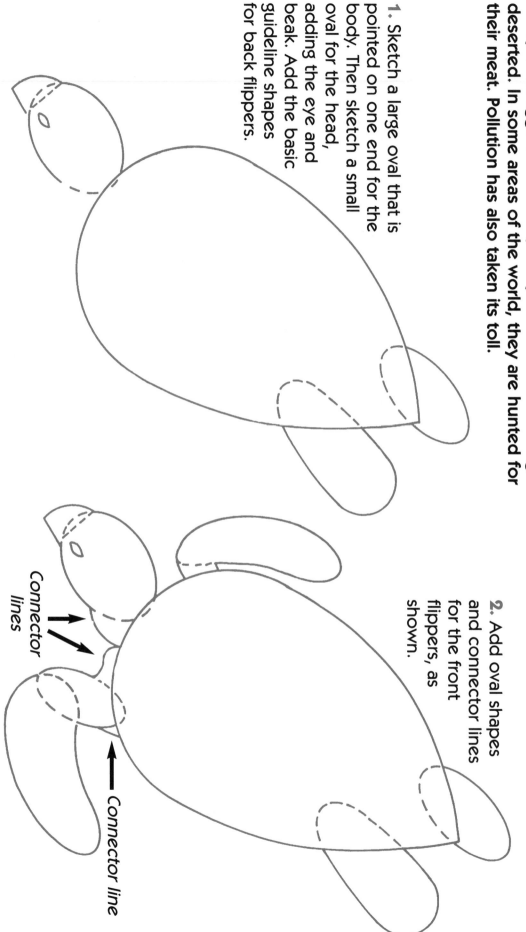

Connector lines

Connector line

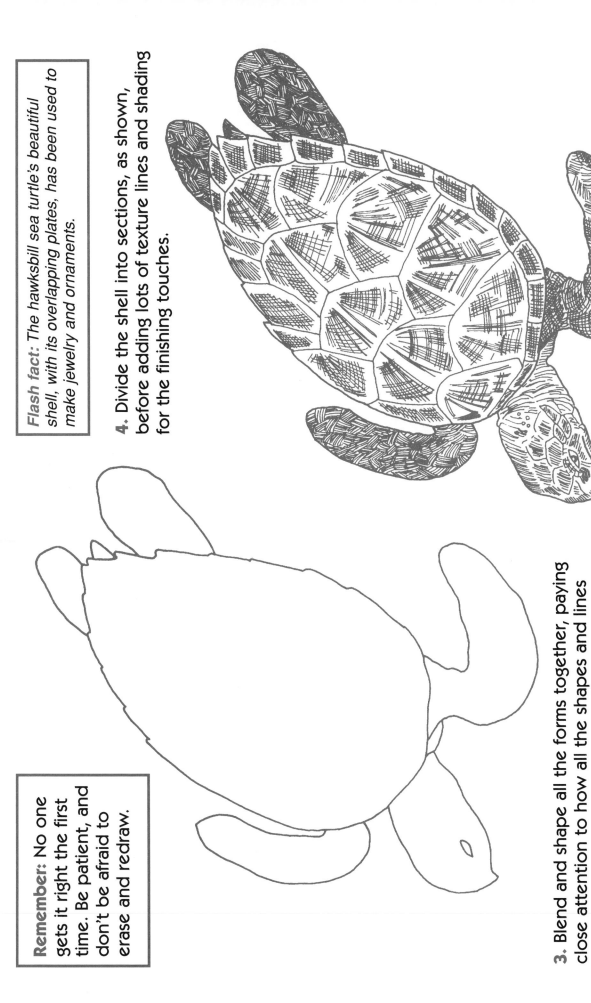

Flash fact: The hawksbill sea turtle's beautiful shell, with its overlapping plates, has been used to make jewelry and ornaments.

4. Divide the shell into sections, as shown, before adding lots of texture lines and shading for the finishing touches.

Remember: No one gets it right the first time. Be patient, and don't be afraid to erase and redraw.

3. Blend and shape all the forms together, paying close attention to how all the shapes and lines interconnect. When you are satisfied with the way your sea turtle looks, start adding details. Note the jagged edges on the outline of the shell.

Bridled wallaby

This small Australian creature is related to the kangaroo. It hops along, sometimes with a baby in its pouch, steadying itself with its long tail. The wallaby hops in an odd way: It whirls its arms around in circles as it jumps.

Remember: Keep all your guidelines lightly drawn, so they will be easier to erase later.

1. Draw a large, egg-shaped oval for the body, angled as shown. Next, add other oval shapes for the head, eyes, nose, and right shoulder. Then, sketch in curved lines for the arms and tiny triangles for the claws.

2. Create the legs and feet with rectangles and triangular guideline shapes. Then add the long, curved tail. Make sure that you have built a solid foundation with the first two steps before continuing.

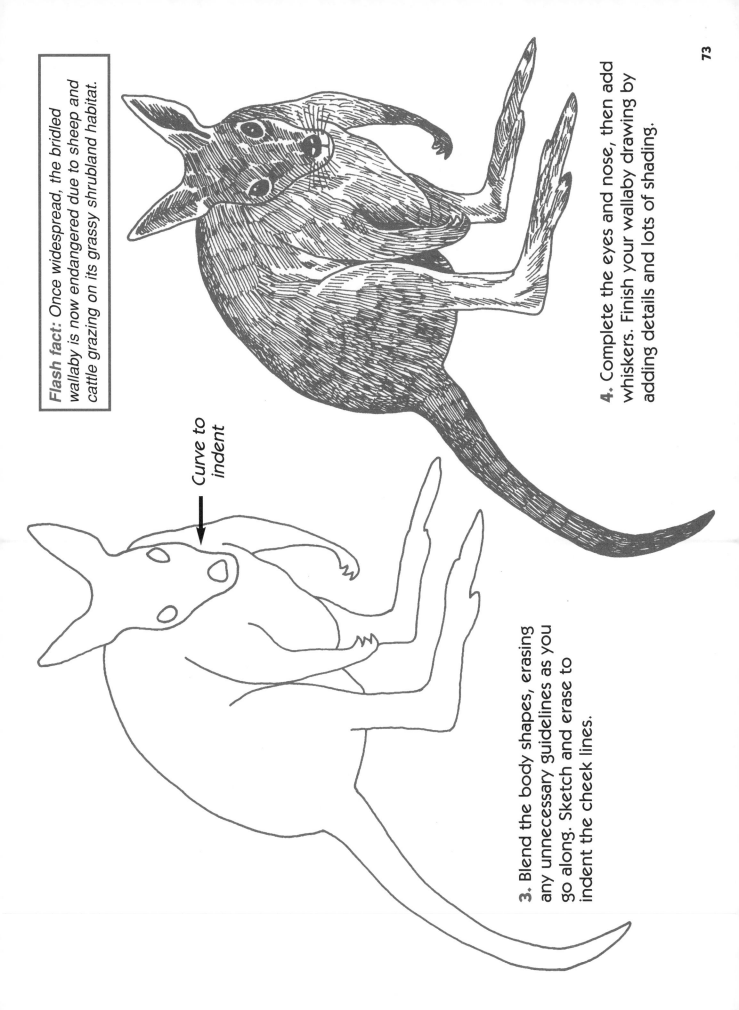

Flash fact: Once widespread, the bridled wallaby is now endangered due to sheep and cattle grazing on its grassy shrubland habitat.

Curve to indent

3. Blend the body shapes, erasing any unnecessary guidelines as you go along. Sketch and erase to indent the cheek lines.

4. Complete the eyes and nose, then add whiskers. Finish your wallaby drawing by adding details and lots of shading.

African Wild Dog

These wild dogs live in packs of up to 30 members and hunt as teams. They have great endurance and will chase their prey until it is exhausted. Many have been killed by farmers who are concerned for their livestock.

1. Begin with a large, free-form oval guideline shape for the body. Add a smaller, overlapping oval for the head and neck. Then, using simple guideline shapes, sketch in the eyes, ears, snout, and nose.

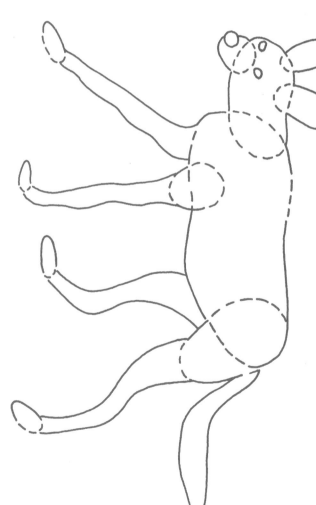

2. Add shapes for the long legs, the paws, and a pointy tail.

4. Add shading and irregular patches of darker color. No two African wild dogs are exactly the same color. They can be black, gray, brown, or any shade in between, and usually have blotches of white, orange, or yellow on their coats.

3. Combine and blend all the shapes and lines together into a smooth outline of the wild dog. Erase any guidelines you no longer need.

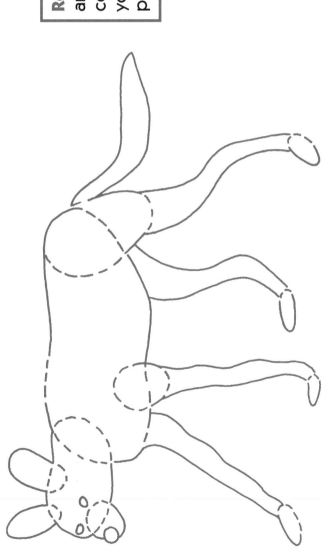

Tuatara

Once mistaken for a lizard, the tuatara is the only remaining member of an entire group of ancient reptiles. The Maori people of New Zealand gave the tuatara its name, which means "peaks on the back."

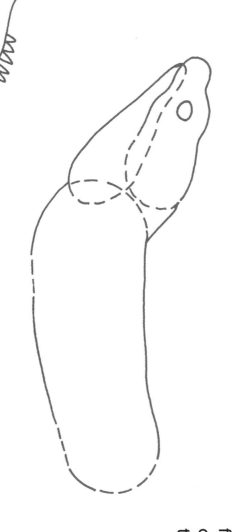

1. Begin with a large, free-form oval for the body. Add two overlapping ovals for the head and connect the top one to the body.

2. Add the long reptilian tail and sketch the guideline shapes for the feet and claws. Then, starting on the head, draw a line of small triangles all the way to the tip of the tail.

Tip: Make sure that you have built a solid foundation with the first two steps before going on to step 3.

Flash fact: Tuataras have been known to live for more than 100 years.

3. Outline the entire body by blending the shapes, erasing any guidelines you no longer need as you go along.

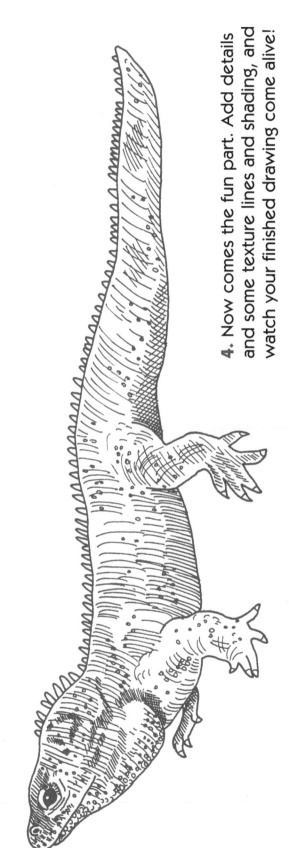

4. Now comes the fun part. Add details and some texture lines and shading, and watch your finished drawing come alive!

Golden Lion Tamarin

The golden lion tamarin has lost much of its habitat in the rain forest of South America. In 1990, only about 450 remained in the wild. By 2002, thanks to protective measures, there were about 1,000.

Tip: Many overlapping shapes are required to complete this picture. Don't let that worry you. No matter how complicated an image appears, you will be able to draw it if you break it down into simple steps.

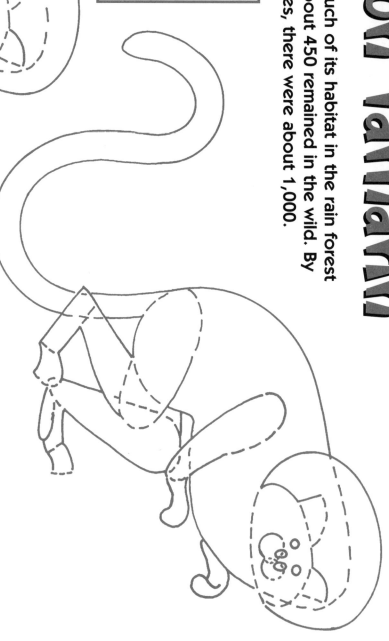

1. Begin with a large free-form guideline shape for the body and an oval for the head. Within that oval, draw another one for the face. Then sketch two triangular ears on top of it.

2. Add guidelines for the eyes, nose, and mouth, then all the additional shapes for the legs and long, flowing tail.

3. Carefully erase any guidelines that you no longer need as you blend and refine the shapes and lines. Pay close attention to the way the mane sits on top of this monkey's head.

4. Complete the facial features. Then add shading and other details to the mane and body. The tamarin's mane is a bright golden orange, which gets darker farther down the body.

Flash fact: Due to successful breeding programs in zoos world-wide, more of these monkeys live in zoos than in the wild.

California Condor

In 2002, the California condor population was 198 worldwide. Most of those birds were being raised in captivity, but 76 of them had been released to the wild. The species is still dangerously close to extinction.

1. Start with a narrow oval guide-line for the body. Add a small oval for the head and a curved triangle for the tail. Connect long, curved lines to the body to form the wings, then add a series of triangles at the end of each wing for feathers.

Connect

Connect

Add triangle

2. Blend all the shapes into one body outline. Erase any guidelines you don't need.

Wavy line

3. Complete this bird by drawing lots of short lines with curved edges to define its body and tail features.

Add eye

Complete beak

Flash fact: With a wingspan of more than 10 feet, a condor can soar effortlessly for hours. It is the largest bird in North America.

Galápagos Tortoise

The giant tortoise exists only in the Galápagos Islands, off the coast of South America. It can grow up to four feet in shell length and weigh 500 pounds or more. It can live up to 200 years—longer than any other animal.

Curved lines

2. Blend the shapes as shown to form a smooth outline of the tortoise.

Small curves for the toes

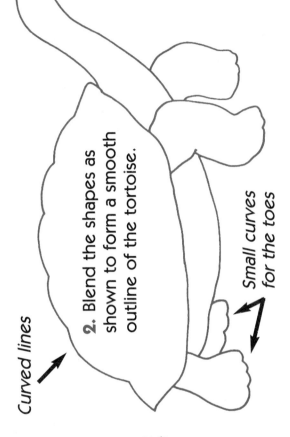

Tip: Focus on one part of the body at a time.

3. Add facial features. Then, to complete your drawing, add the shell pattern, skin texture, and some background scenery.

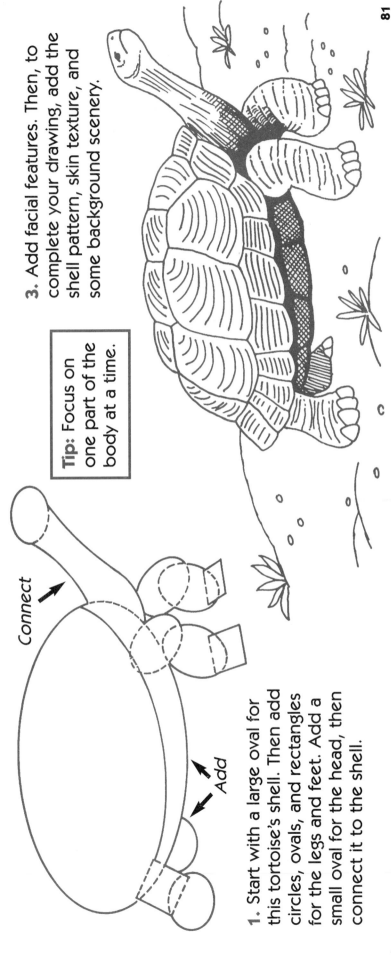

Connect

Add

1. Start with a large oval for this tortoise's shell. Then add circles, ovals, and rectangles for the legs and feet. Add a small oval for the head, then connect it to the shell.

Right whale

The right whale got its name from whalers, because for them it was the "right" whale to hunt. It lives close to the shore, is a slow swimmer, and contains lots of oil.

1. Start with a large, lightly drawn oval guideline shape for the body and a smaller one for the front fin. Add a small eye and a roughly rectangular shape for the head. Then sketch lines to connect the head to the body.

2. Draw this whale's tail by first sketching two wavy triangular shapes joined at the bottom. Connect this shape to the rear of the body. Then add long curvy lines on the front of the whale as guide-lines for the mouth.

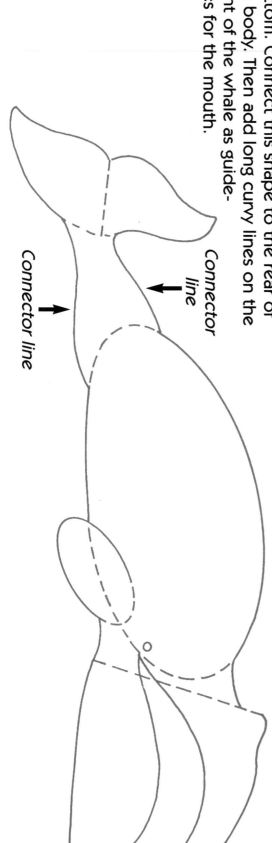

Connector line

Connector line

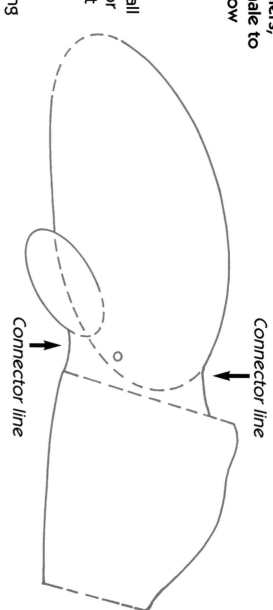

Connector line

Connector line

Remember: Draw all guidelines lightly in steps 1 and 2, so they will be easier to change or erase later.

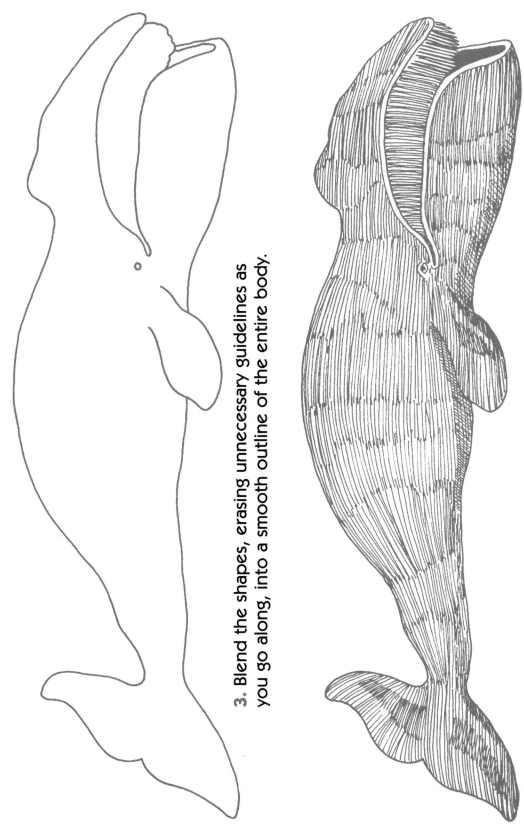

Flash fact: Like other baleen whales, the right whale has two blow-holes. When it comes up for air, it blows out water in two directions.

3. Blend the shapes, erasing unnecessary guidelines as you go along, into a smooth outline of the entire body.

4. Add light, horizontal shading along the body. Use straight vertical lines to draw the baleen in the whale's mouth. The baleen acts like a filter, sifting tiny sea creatures from the water for the whale to eat.

Whooping Crane

These cranes live in the marshlands of North America. By 1941, hunting and marsh drainage had reduced their numbers in the wild to fewer than 20.

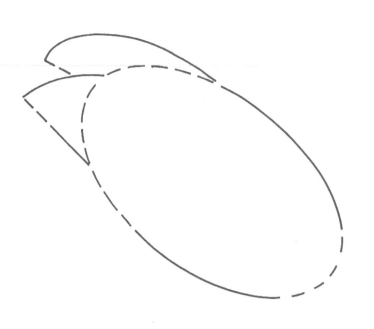

1. Start by drawing a large oval for the body. Then draw the two basic shapes for the tail feathers.

2. Sketch an oval for the head and add a triangle for the beak. Connect the head to the body, forming the long, slender neck. Note how one of the connecting lines extends to the right leg. Add the long legs and use a series of triangles to create the feet.

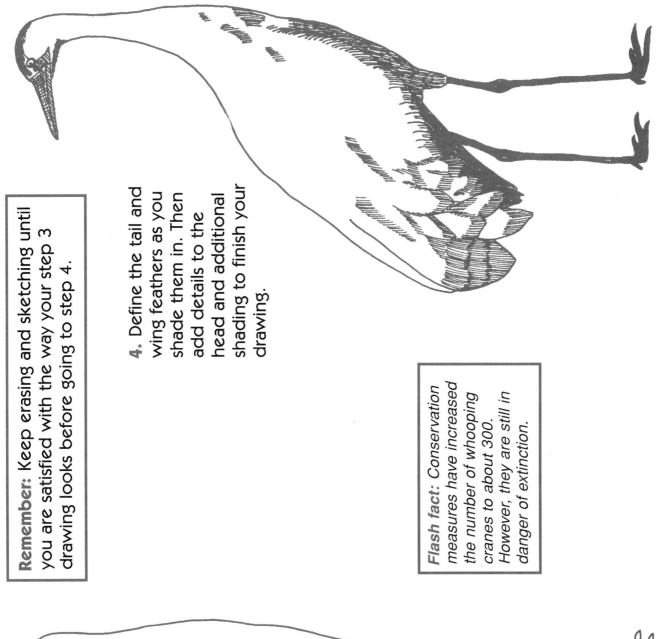

Remember: Keep erasing and sketching until you are satisfied with the way your step 3 drawing looks before going to step 4.

4. Define the tail and wing feathers as you shade them in. Then add details to the head and additional shading to finish your drawing.

Flash fact: Conservation measures have increased the number of whooping cranes to about 300. However, they are still in danger of extinction.

3. Sketch and erase to blend the shapes into a smooth outline of this bird's body.

Orangutan

The trees of Borneo and Sumatra—home to the orangutan—are being cut down for timber. As the forests disappear, so do the orangutans.

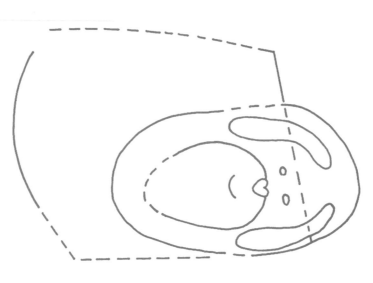

Tip: Sometimes a drawing may seem too hard to do. Just break it down, step by step, into simple guideline shapes. With practice, you will soon be able to draw any animal, now matter how difficult it seems at first.

1. Begin with a basic oval shape for the head. Within it, draw a smaller one. Add the eyes, mouth, and a small heart-shaped nose. Then sketch two long, curving ovals on either sides of the eyes. Next, for the body, draw a boxy shape with a curved bottom.

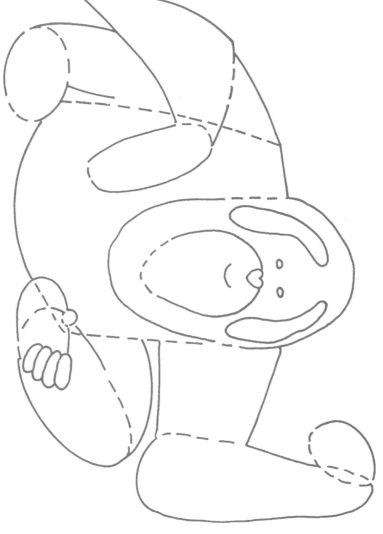

2. Carefully add guideline shapes for the arms, hands, legs, and feet. There are a lot of overlapping shapes here, so take your time, sketching the limbs lightly, one at a time, until you have it right.

3. Combine and blend the shapes into an outline drawing of this ape. Note how the outline is rippled in some places to represent the orangutan's shaggy body.

Flash fact: In the language spoken on the island of Borneo, orangutan means "man who lives in the forest."

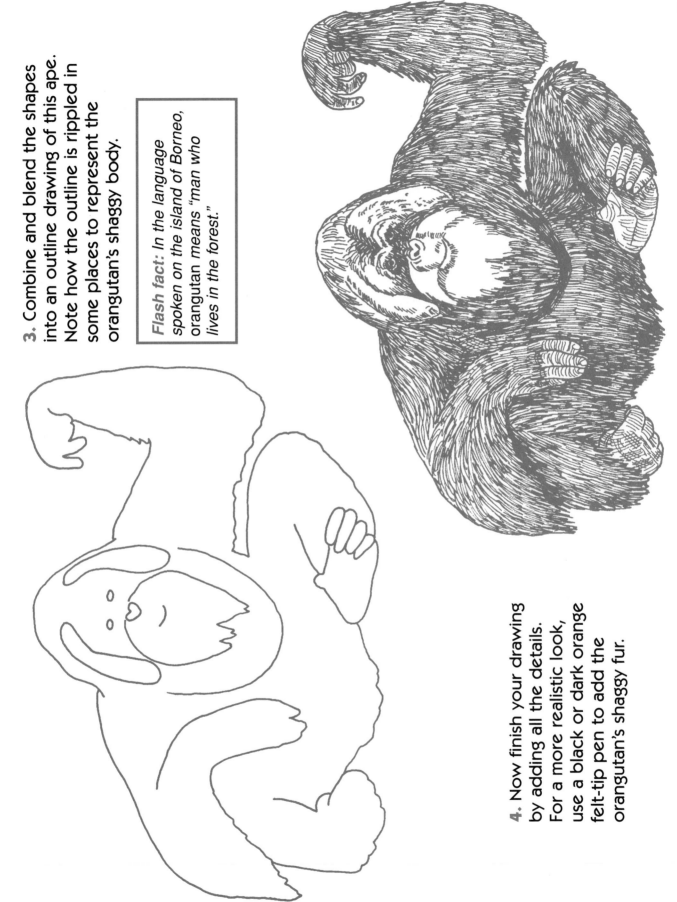

4. Now finish your drawing by adding all the details. For a more realistic look, use a black or dark orange felt-tip pen to add the orangutan's shaggy fur.

Clouded Leopard

This big, yellowish-gray cat lives in the forests and swamps of Asia. It hunts by night, but also is hunted by humans for its beautiful spotted coat.

1. Begin with three basic oval shapes for the head, shoulder, and rump. Connect them, then add guideline shapes for the ears, snout, and mouth.

2. Add guideline shapes for the legs, paw, and tail.

Remember: Dotted lines indicate guidelines that you will change or erase as your drawing progresses.

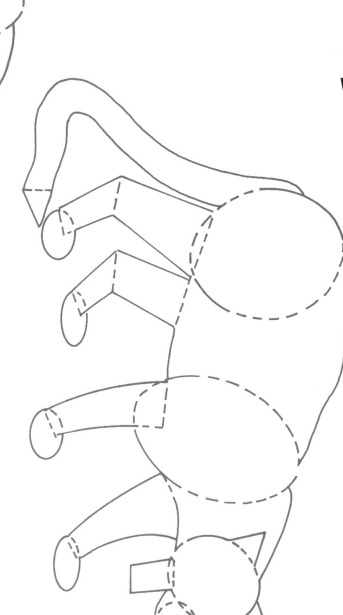

3. Blend and shape all the forms, paying close attention to how all the shapes and lines interconnect. When you are satisfied with the way the body outline looks, start adding details.

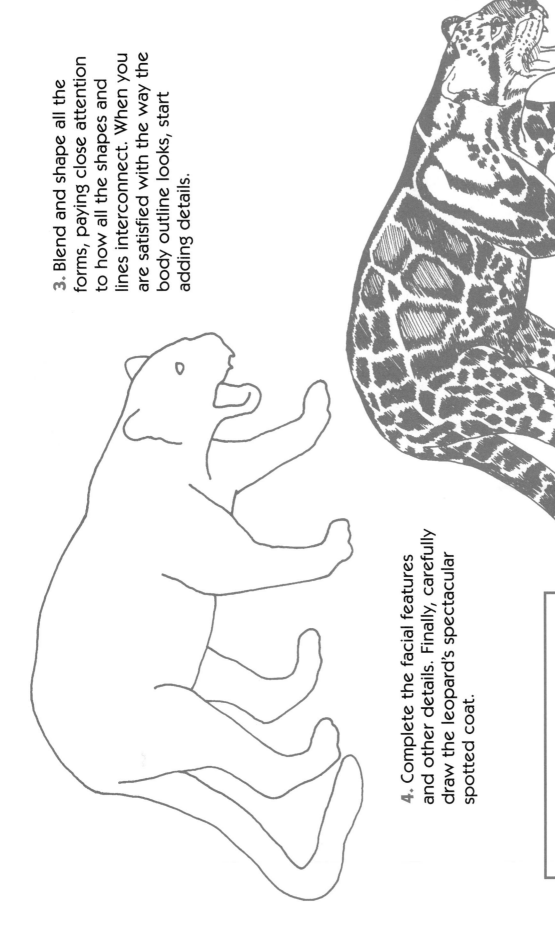

4. Complete the facial features and other details. Finally, carefully draw the leopard's spectacular spotted coat.

Flash fact: This cat has especially long canine teeth and a fierce look, but cannot roar. The clouded leopard is a purring cat.

Estuarine Saltwater Crocodile

Long hunted for its valuable hide, this crocodile can grow as long as 23 feet. It is the world's biggest reptile. Now protected, it can be found all over southeastern Asia.

> **Remember:** Don't be afraid to erase! No one gets it right the first time.

1. Start your sketch with a large free-form oval for this crocodile's body. Next, add a smaller overlapping oval for the thick neck. Then add basic shapes for the head and jaws, and a small circle for the eye.

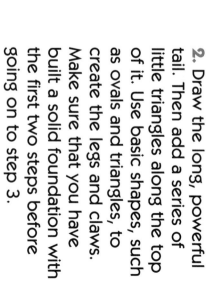

2. Draw the long, powerful tail. Then add a series of little triangles along the top of it. Use basic shapes, such as ovals and triangles, to create the legs and claws. Make sure that you have built a solid foundation with the first two steps before going on to step 3.

Flash fact: Northern Australia is one of the few places where crocodile populations are increasing.

4. Complete the eye and head. Note the bumpy ridges running along this crocodile's back. Finally, add lots of scales, textures, and shading to complete your drawing.

3. Combine all the shapes, erasing guidelines as you go along. The goal is to create a smooth, clean outline of this animal's body. Once you are satisfied with your drawing, you will be ready to add the finishing touches.

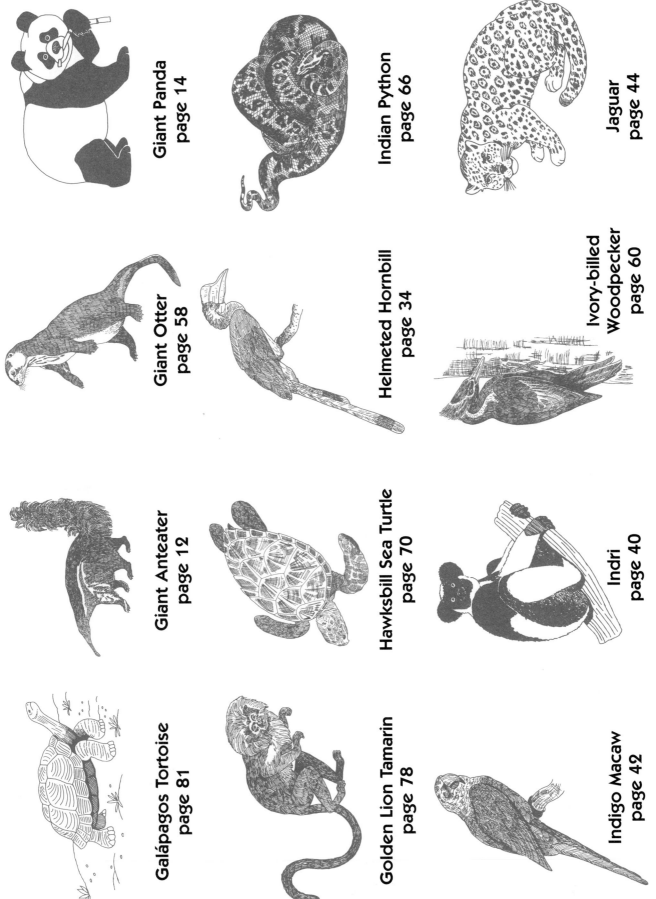

Giant Panda
page 14

Indian Python
page 66

Jaguar
page 44

Giant Otter
page 58

Helmeted Hornbill
page 34

Ivory-billed
Woodpecker
page 60

Giant Anteater
page 12

Hawksbill Sea Turtle
page 70

Indri
page 40

Galápagos Tortoise
page 81

Golden Lion Tamarin
page 78

Indigo Macaw
page 42

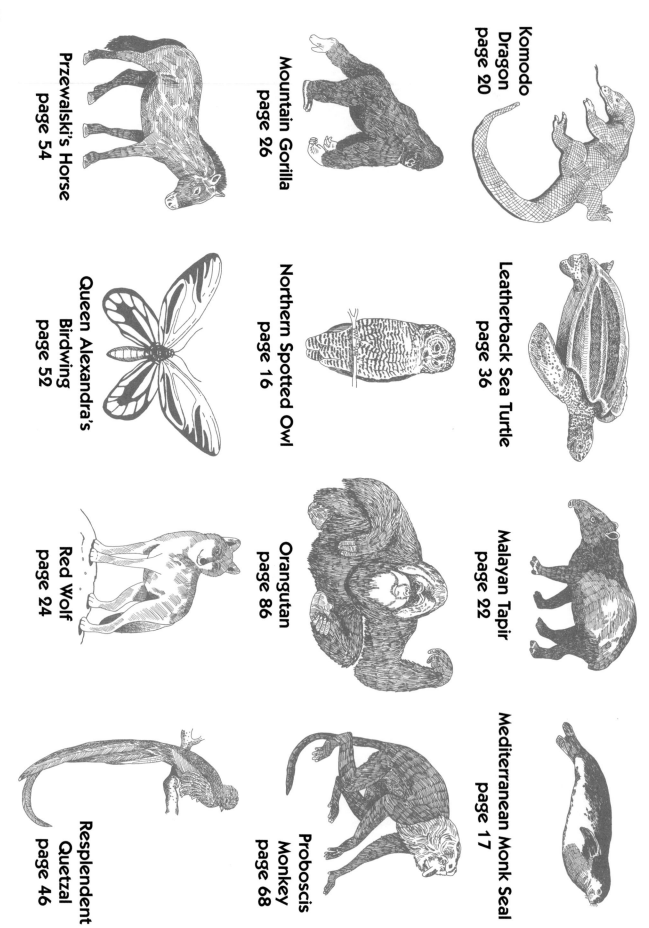

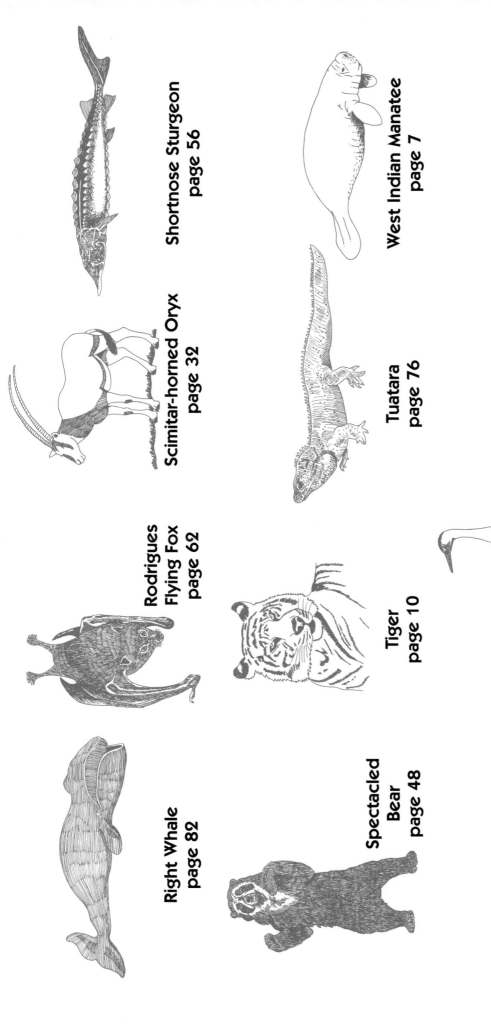

Shortnose Sturgeon
page 56

West Indian Manatee
page 7

Scimitar-horned Oryx
page 32

Tuatara
page 76

**Rodrigues
Flying Fox**
page 62

Tiger
page 10

Whooping Crane
page 84

Right Whale
page 82

**Spectacled
Bear**
page 48